A MERRY
MEMOIR
OF
SEX,
DEATH
&
RELIGION

Daniel C. Maguire

Caritas Communications Caritas Thiensville, Wisconsin
Communications

A Merry Memoir of Sex, Death, and Religion

Daniel C. Maguire

Dedication

To The American Association

of University Professors,

which stands tall as the brilliant and committed

guardian of the integrity of the academe.

A Merry Memoir of Sex, Death, and Religion

Maguire, Daniel C, S.T.D.

A Merry Memoir of Sex, Death, and Religion

Caritas Communications

Thiensville, Wisconsin 53092

dgawlik@wi.rr.com

414.531.0503

Table Of Contents

A Merry Memoir of Sex, Death, and Religion

Daniel C. Maguire

"Life is serious all the time, but living cannot be.
You may have all the solemnity you wish in your neckties,
but in anything important (such as sex, death, and religion),
you must have mirth or you will have madness."

G. K. Chesterton, Lunacy and Letters,
edited by Dorothy Collins
(New York: Sheed and Ward, 1958), p. 97.

A Merry Memoir of Sex, Death, and Religion

CHAPTER ONE
OVERTURE

The year was 1949.

It happened on the corner of Ardleigh Street and Evergreen Avenue. That's where the mailbox was. I hesitated one little second and then dropped in my application to enter St. Charles Seminary in Overbrook, Philadelphia. I was 18 and I wanted to be a priest.

No surprise. Of the four sons in my family, only one did not become a priest. We were an Irish, Catholic, priestly people. I knew the price-tag was steep. I was volunteering for a lifetime of unending obedience and absolutely no sexual pleasure. I had already stopped masturbating. I knew that was key. The church sensed that if you couldn't keep your hands off yourself, you probably couldn't keep them off others. So the just-say-no-to-sex thing was the entry fee and I was ready to pay it. I learned later that instructions from Rome said that no seminarian who had masturbated within six months of ordination to the priesthood should be ordained. The rule was rigid. One seminarian translated it into blunt language: "Pecker-pullers need not apply."

Somehow it did not strike us as beyond odd that the untouchable penis was also a *sine qua non* for getting in the front door of the seminary. Girls, lacking this instrumentation, were barred. Whatever!

Lots of people wanted to be priests in those days, at least lots of Irish Americans did. A priest in the family was a major distinction. There is an Irish song about a new bride who made a great match because her husband had "a house and a cow and a brother a priest." How do you top that! For Italian American Catholics it was different. An Italian American friend of mine toyed with the idea of becoming a priest and announced his pious plans to his father. I was shocked to my Irish toes when he told me his father's response: "You want to be a priest and not get married ever in your life? What kind of a fuckin' Italian are you?" I knew then that Italians were a faithless people and that when I was a priest I would have to do a lot of apostolic work on them...little suspecting the kind of work they were going to do on me.

Over a hundred of us showed up for the entrance exam to the seminary. It was a buyer's market in those days for Catholic seminaries. We all knew that half of us would be rejected and sent back into the lowly realm of the laity. It was one tough test. I remember one of the questions was: "What are the two principal lakes in Nicaragua?" I took a stab with the only two words I had for that country, both derived from a then-popular song. My answer: "Lake Managua and Lake Nicaragua." To this day I don't know if those are the two main lakes down there, but I did make the cut.

The Philadelphia seminary was known as "the West Point of Catholic Seminaries." The discipline was strict. Of course it did save me from lung cancer. No smoking was permitted. If you were found with tobacco in your possession you would be dismissed. Like everyone then I had started to smoke a bit and that ended as I stepped onto the seminary grounds.

I look back on my classmates at that time entering that Spartan world…young, earnest, bright, (experts on Nicaraguan lakes and the like), idealistic, eager to serve people in the church, ready to bend their wills to the grim discipline, rising at 5:00 a.m., to bed at 9:00 p.m., eating many meals in silence while holy books were read to us. One would have to wonder where we came from.

Parochial is where we came from.

Catholics of that era did not have to settle out in the country and wear different dress like the Amish people or Hasidic Jews. We achieved the same cult effect right in the city. We imperiously rewrote geography. In Philadelphia, Catholics did not live in Germantown, Manyunk, Mount Airy, or South Philly or anywhere else. Of course they did live in all those places, but they were parochially renamed. Instead we lived in Our Mother of Consolation, or Holy Cross, or St. Bridget's parish. "He married a girl from St. Bernard's parish and then they moved to Our Lady of Loreto." "I was born in St. Martin's parish but grew up in St. Monica's." Catholic ghettoes did not need walls.

Marrying someone who was not a Catholic was a "mixed marriage," and barred from the usual wedding solemnities in church. The wedding took place in the sterile office of the pastor's residence. The non-Catholic (usually some brand of Protestant) had to promise to raise all the children Catholic (a stipulation still in force) or it was a no-go. Marrying a Jew? Well I didn't know anyone who did such a thing back then! Catholics knew better than to fall in love with Jews. (We knew that Jesus was a Jew but that was different.)

Most of us grew up without Jewish friends. Not my brother-in-law Frank. He lived in West Oak Lane in a rather Jewish neighborhood. When he got into first grade and found out the absolute necessity of baptism he was also informed that Jews didn't have it. Alarmed for the perilous state of his little friends, Frank rushed home to correct that. He gathered his five close Jewish friends in his back yard, convinced them handily that they really, really needed it, turned the hose on lightly and baptized each one of them in the name of the Father and of the Son, and of the Holy Ghost. A quick fix. How these kids reported this salvific intervention when they returned home that day we never did learn. Frank was afterwards known in his family as Frank the Baptist.

Would You Marry a Non-Catholic?

There were two kinds of people in that world: Catholic and Non-Catholics. The stress on Catholics over the Non's was at times extreme, as in the Catholic newspaper headline: "No Catholics Killed in Oklahoma Storm." My nephew Bernard did a variation on this, dividing people into Catholics and Publics, referring to the schools they attended. When watching a game on TV he would check out various players asking his mother if this one or that one was "a Catholic or a Public." It was important to know.

Of course as far as sports went it was never necessary to be out on the field bumping into Non-Catholics or Publics. There were Catholic sports leagues, the CYO's, Catholic Youth Organizations. In Philadelphia in its Catholic heyday, every Catholic child could get twelve years of Catholic schooling free. Costs were paid by the collections in the parishes. (On top of that there were Catholic colleges and the Archbishop of Philadelphia, former Notre Dame president Cardinal O'Hara, said it was a mortal sin for Catholics to enroll elsewhere. The University of Pennsylvania, Temple, and Drexel were no-go-zones.) There were Catholic leagues in all sports and Catholic championships where we could play our hearts out with no fear of heretical contamination. You could play football for years and never tackle a Public.

Notre Dame and Bing Crosby

Above all else in the world was Notre Dame football. This was not a game; this was sacramental Catholicism in full flower! (Forget that some of

4

their players were Publics!) I remember the old Sulpician priest, Fr. Mc-Cormick. Fortunately he is now dead, given Notre Dame's football humiliations of recent years. As he put it to me once: "Protestants may criticize the Catholic church as much as they like but when Notre Dame's football team is out there on that field, they can't deny that." A good point, I guess. His thought seemed to be, forget theology. Notre Dame's success on the football field was all the warranty for the faith that we needed. Of course for this form of apologetics to silence and fell those Protestant critics, Notre Dame had to win. Otherwise what kind of message was God sending? Poor Fr. McCormick. When Notre Dame would lose, he walked in the shadow of death and depression for a week. His faith itself seemed imperiled. Notre Dame, since they are not number one right now, has been doing as much losing as winning. That would have driven Fr. McCormick to his death—if not into outright atheism.

When we were in elementary school, we had our own way of explaining Notre Dame losses. *Protestant referees!*

At that time it was not just in the Catholic world that being a priest was super-high on the prestige scale. Even the heretics in Hollywood played along with Catholic status norms. "Going My Way" and "The Bells of St. Mary's" showed priests and nuns as mavens of virtue and sweetness, and some like Bing Crosby could even sing. You could make fun of Elmer Gantry, but touch not my anointed priests. It was a really cool time for Catholics.

Priests and Mothers and Such

We young idealists stepping into the seminaries were not unaware of the social heights to which we aspired. Mothers played a big role. Being "the mother of a priest" was a pinnacle experience. (The father of a priest, in a clear bit of sexism, got little or no credit.) When a priest was ordained, his hands were anointed as the bishop intoned: "What these hands bless is truly blessed and what these hands consecrate is truly consecrated." The anointed hands

5

were then wrapped in a linen *manutergium*. The *manutergium* was later given to his mother and when she died, her hands were wrapped in that sanctified linen. Anyone could guess that this was a ticket straight into heaven. Indeed mothers were so much into the priest-son-thing that I often dared to wonder if it was they who had the calling to the priesthood, and the sons were just surrogates. Aside from the social prestige, a priest's mother did not lose her son to another woman. Home for him was still her home. A win-win deal.

Awards were given in those days to "the Catholic mother of the year." (Again, alas, no similar prize for hyper-Catholic dads.) Prize-winning, fertile Catholic mothers of the year always had in their overflowing brood three or four priests and a couple of nuns for full measure. Breeding so many celibates was in a strange way a form of population control if those young rascals stayed faithful to their vows, but that was not the goal in mind in priest-making.

My own decision to enter the priesthood was not mother driven. In fact, Cassie as we all called her, wasn't too keen on it to my great disappointment. She didn't resist but there was a noticeable lack of enthusiasm. Of course, she had done the priest thing twice already. When my brother Pat was ordained in 1940 it gave my mother a swollen hand. So many enthused Irish parishioners were pumping her hand the day of his First Mass that her hand puffed up. The same honorific suffering beset her five years later when Joe was ordained.

She admitted to me in later years that she had hopes that I would be a doctor. At the same time I've guessed that this very bright lady sensed I would not be a good fit in the world of priestly discipline. My father didn't push me either. As a young man back in Glenties, County Donegal, he entered the seminary and lasted only thirty days. He was so anxious to get out, he would not even wait two more days when there would be a train. He walked the 35 miles back to his home in Glenties, County Donegal. Thoughts of the young Cassie whom he already knew may have spurred that long walk. "I knew if I couldn't marry Cassie I wouldn't marry anybody," he said later. I was bred of love and that's a good start.

A Priestly Kid

I didn't need a parental push to get me to the seminary door. Priesthood was the only thing bigger than Notre Dame football. In fact I started my own church at age seven. I installed myself as priest and started out with a small but richly diversified congregation. There was Teresa, my sister, who found my sermons fun. Next there was Jean Greer, who often lived with us while her parents were away at work with the Stotesbury family, who had houses in Palm Beach and in Bar Harbor, Maine as well as in Philadelphia. Jean was an interesting congregant since she was Presbyterian, a Non-Catholic, a Public. (My parish was more ecumenical than the church at that point in history.) My parents faithfully sent Jean to her own church on Sundays and Jean brought that experience back to my liturgies. She was annoyingly critical of my sermons. "You don't shout enough, Danny!" she would say—right in the middle of my fervent homily. Apparently she had a fairly boisterous minister at the time and I paled in comparison. Still she always showed up and that was all an aspiring young church maker could hope for. The third and final member of my congregation was my cat, Judy Boy. (I named the cat Judy when I got it and was later informed of its male gender. I kept the Judy and added Boy. That took care of it.) Judy Boy was my most faithful friend and congregant and never criticized my sermons. Of course, he didn't purr during them either. Still he was the best behaved member of my congregation.

Soon, however, tragedy struck. My fledgling little church was crushed by ecclesiastical authority in the person of my mother. Since I was offering a full-service parish, I wanted it to have all the fixin's. On the feast of St. Blaise, the patron saint of throats (sore or otherwise), it was customary to have your throat blessed. In more conventional churches this was done by having two unlit candles tied at the base into a V shape. These candles were then held to your throat as the priest said the appropriate prayer to this medically specialized saint. (St. Blaise was not an 'ear, nose, and throat' guy: just throats).

Well I had no candles, so what's a seven-year-old priest to do? In a display of ritual adaptiveness, I got two steak knives and attached them just as was done with the candles in the other competing, candle-endowed Catholic churches. Voila! With that done, I proceeded with the blessings: the Catholic's throat, the Presbyterian's throat, and Judy Boy's throat were duly blessed and none of them to my best recollection ever suffered throat maladies thereafter. This liturgical effort did not shut down my mission since my mother did not learn of it til later.

What did me in was the marbles. Since I didn't have anything like those little communion wafers, I decided to use marbles. I didn't offer any to Judy Boy since he didn't like to be hand fed, and anyhow, I realized he had never even been baptized. Jean and Teresa did take the marbles and happily spit them out in a hurry. That's when my mother happened upon the service and my promising little ministry crashed. My first collision with ecclesiastical authority! More would follow. Maybe my later entrance into the priesthood was a little bit of get-even with Cassie who had so peremptorily suppressed my earlier creative work in ministry.

The Sin Thing

Catholics have always been big on sin detection and sin confession. This began at age seven, when, it was claimed, you acquired "the use of reason." I actually think that "the use of reason" comes way after adolescence, and maybe not until middle age, and sometimes not at all. That's why there are so many Republicans. Anyway, that's what they decided back then. At seven reason kicked in. And, obviously, it followed as the night the day, if you could reason you could sin.

So seven was the age of First Confession and First Communion. To confess you had to have sins. At seven the biggies were disobedience, cursing, and fighting with siblings. If it was confession day and you had neither cursed nor disobeyed and had been patient at home, you had a problem. When you arrived in church for confession you would first kneel for a final "examination of conscience." Once my eight-year-old niece DeeDee was with me and we both knelt to examine what depravity we had fallen into the previous week. After a minute of this, DeeDee poked me and announced in a panic, "Uncle Danny, I don't got no sins!" Since she was the youngest of seven I urged that she must have gotten mad at one of them. She beamed with relief. "I did," she said with a big happy smile, and that little sinner was on her way. I've since suggested to her that moment wrote her epitaph. *Here Lies Edith "I don't got no sins!" Gallagher Boyd.*

Of course, finding sins got easier when the hormones kicked in. We were taught that any sexual thoughts, words, or deeds were sins, and not just little "venial sins"; they were "mortal sins," the kind that could cast you into the fires of hell for all eternity if you died unrepentant. Sexual thoughts and feelings would occur; that was conceded. They didn't become sins until you "entertained" them. If you didn't banish them but deliberately "entertained" them and enjoyed them, you sinned, and you sinned big time! So if in confession you admitted to "impure thoughts" the priest would then ask: "Did you entertain them?" I always wanted to say "No, they entertained me," but I knew that would not get me the needed absolution.

There was an Italian priest, right from Italy, who was kindly and gentle and he always had the longest lines for confession. Partly that was due to the fact that his English was poor and folks discovered that he didn't understand half of what he was hearing. It was great. You could pour out your sordid doings, and with a wave of his priestly hand and a three Hail Mary penance you were back on the street as clean as a whistle. We all hoped his English would not improve too quickly.

Excommunication!

Private sins could be forgiven but there were big sins that could knock you right out of the church. I remember an early scandal in our parish, Our Mother of Consolation. There was no consolation for Chick Breen. Chick's marriage broke up. Two years later he met and fell in love with another woman. In the rules of that day, he could not marry her, until his first wife would die. "Until death do us part" was the marriage promise. So Chick and his lady married "outside the church" which meant they were, in the jargon of the day, "living in sin." We didn't put public sinners in the stocks. We didn't need such props. Chick was effectively stigmatized, marked with the sin sign. We had our own form of "shunning." We viewed Chick with something between fear and awe since he was a witness to the terrible power of lust. We pitied him too because he was not part of the church. An aura of forbiddenness and uncleanness hung over him. He was there, but he was not there. Excommunicated was the word. I was about twelve years old at that time and I remember all of those emotions whenever I would see Chick.

Then one day something happened that I have never forgotten. I was an altar boy and I went to the church during the week on some altar boy mission. The church was empty as I entered, or, at least I had thought it was. As I started up the aisle I suddenly became aware of a man kneeling and bent over in the very last pew. It was Chick and he was quietly sobbing. Chick did not live long. Only much later did I decide that we had killed him. Here was a man split by his opposing loves. He loved this church and all of its hopes and consolations, its liturgies and social warmth. He loved this woman and would stick by her. It was too much. Only death could free him from the dilemma and to this day I believe it did.

Later, when as a theologian I concluded that the "no divorce" thing was an ideal, not a club to smash people with and ruin their lives, depriving them of a second chance, I gave credit to Chick. Theory is largely autobiography and his pain was my early teacher.

Communion Time

We all got dressed up for First Communion and marched in procession into the church. We were, one and all, in "a state of grace" since we had been cleansed of our sins in confession the previous day. The common think then was that when you received communion Jesus was physically present inside of you. I asked the nun how long that lasted. Her guesstimate was about an hour before the digestive processes sent Jesus away. When I got home I checked the clock and realized he was still there inside me so I started running up and down the stairs. This annoyed my mother and she asked me what I was doing. I wondered why she would ask. My reply: "I'm giving Our Lord a ride." I was just being hospitable. My faith was pure.

Catholic Politics

When the Irish arrived in America, their first three tasks were to find the nearest church, the nearest pub, and the headquarters of the Democratic party. You would no more vote Republican than you would cheer for Southern Methodist's football team. I remember going to church with my uncle Pat one time right after an election. One of his friends joined us and told uncle Pat that he had it on good authority that a fellow parishioner Michael McCoy had voted Republican the previous Tuesday. Uncle Pat's shocked reply: "How in God's name could that be! Sure I saw him at Mass last Sunday!" I learned early on that voting Republican was one of the worst things you could do, probably worse than masturbation. In fact one of my friends opined that Republicans were all chronic masturbators and that was what made them the way they were. That might explain it, but to be fair, we really had no evidence.

Catholics Need Not Apply

Of course the tight knitting of the Catholic community was helped by a lot of good old American anti-Catholicism. Unlike Donegal where the Protestants were few and unobtrusive, this country was rife with them.

Once in Boston a factory put up a sign advertising for more workers. It included the ominous notation: Catholics Need Not Apply. A waggish Catholic scribbled in a couplet on the bottom of the sign:

Who ever wrote this wrote it well

For the same is written on the gates of hell!

We loved stories where Catholic wit triumphed over Protestant oppression. There was a story that made the rounds ,of a priest talking to a mixed audience and defending the truths of the Catholic faith. A man rose and asked: "Do you have the proof of those statements with you?" The priest replied that he did not but that he could get it. The man retorted: "Well then in the absence of proof do you mind if I call you a liar?"

The priest replied: "Not at all. Do you have your parents' marriage certificate with you?" The man said: "Of course not." Said the priest, "then in the absence of proof, do you mind if I call you a bastard?" As good as a Notre Dame victory that was!

All this animosity and strangeness did get Catholic voters to the polls and into politics. Catholic mayors were commonplace and were loyally supported by the Catholic population, even in a few cases while those mayors had found their way into jail. You could overlook a lot to keep Catholics in charge. Anyhow, it was probably some Protestant judge that put the poor man behind bars.

Prohibition

Prohibition was good for the Catholics. At least it was good for my father. He quickly mastered the art of beer-making and set up a little brewery in our basement. Business was brisk. It was an Irish neighborhood and even the cops were among my father's steady customers. I loved this. I was just a little fellow and when the men came for beer, I would go to the cellar with them and they would often give me a few drops of beer in a shot glass. Pretty heady stuff for a little guy.

The business thrived until the fateful call came in from the police station. It was the police Sargent, one of my father's steady customers. "I have bad news for you, Barney. You have a bad neighbor and he turned you in. We'll have to come for you. When would be a good time?" It was to be a very friendly arrest. A few hours later two police officers arrived. I was delighted to see them since I knew them well and I asked: "Do you want some beer?" They patted my head gently and sadly said, "No, we have to go somewhere with your Dad." Off went Dad to the jail where he spent the night.

In a remarkable, truly stunning coincidence that proved that there could be justice for Catholics even in Protestant America, Prohibition was repealed the very next day and my father walked! It worked for me too since my brother Barney converted the beer-making apparatus into root beer production and I got more than a few drops of that. Of course, with the switch to root beer the customer list changed. No more Irish cops. But Prohibition did help our family of nine through the Depression. (The Depression was probably also caused by Protestants.)

Prohibition was a telling lesson in American politics for us. It also confirmed the truth of our Catholic faith since Prohibition came out of Protestant uptightness. Didn't Hilaire Belloc have it right when he wrote:

Wherever a Catholic sun doth shine

There's always laughter and good red wine!

At least I always found it so

Benedicamus Domino!

13

The Benedictine monks, who did more than pray, produced Benedictine liqueur. And don't forget Christian Brothers Brandy. Who ever heard of a Presbyterian brandy or a Methodist liqueur! There was even a prayer in the Catholic liturgy, *benedictio cervesii*, a blessing for beer!

Catholics may have been a bit grim on the sex thing but they never condemned booze or bingo. Give them credit for that. "A wee bit of the drink purifies society," my father used to say. "Whiskey" after all is a word derived from the Irish language meaning the "water of life." Having named it, the Irish ever did it homage.

So the Protestant Prohibition was a flop and it gave us Catholic youth an insight into the flawed Protestant character. My brothers Pat, Joe, and Barney used to caddy during Prohibition at a big Republican Protestant country club. (Another *Catholics Need Not Apply*.) They reported back how, at regular intervals, the long fairway at the fifth hole would be cleared and a little plane would arrive from Canada loaded with the forbidden liquid fruit. It was quickly unloaded, it took off, and play resumed. This showed us that these Protestants could drink like a bunch of Catholics when they got behind closed doors. Hypocrites, not honest drinkers they were!

The Depression

Most of our neighbors were "on relief" during the Depression. We narrowly avoided it, to the great pride of my parents. My father had a way of finding easy jobs that involved minimal physical exertion. He had one at Stotesbury's Philadelphia estate, as a night watchman. Do a few rounds, punch a few clocks, drink tea in between and that was a night's work. For a while Mr. Stotesbury kept on a lot of workers who had little to do. Some would diligently shovel the sand out of one of the sand pits on the golf course one day and return it to the same pit the next day. In such company my father was quite at home. But then the Stotesburys took a mean turn and laid off a bunch of people, including my father. That was the first time my brother Joe saw my mother, an "unsinkable Molly Brown," break down and cry. Jean Greer's Presbyterian mother Mabel was there when the news of Dad's firing arrived and my mother was gripped with desperation. I was a newborn babe at the time but my brother Joe remembers Mabel's response to my mother. It was a firm: "We'll never let you starve, Cassie!" They decided to board Jean with us, and that was income.

Mabel was Cassie's closest woman friend and to the end of her life she said of her: "Mabel's the best Christian I ever met." That inserted a bit of saving cognitive dissonance into the Maguire family. With all the negative vibes on Protestants suffusing the Catholic air, our dearest friends, the Greers, were Protestants and the best Christians our sainted mother ever met.

In her nineties, Cassie would reflect on those early days and how Jean's boarding money was the buffer in between Dad's jobs. With a bit of uncharacteristic vulgarity she would say: "'Twas Jean put the ass in us!" Again, in another display of my underappreciated epitaphing skills, I've suggested to Jean that her tombstone should read: *Here Lies Jean Greer Zeiter: She put the ass in the Maguires.* Cemeteries could do with a bit of whimsy.

Seminary Life

Seminary sounds an awful lot like *cemetery*, and there were similarities. Lots of bodies and lots of silence. Still we laughed a lot and were encouraged to play a lot of sports. They knew we had to do something with our bodies and good clean sports were the answer.

Answers. Answers were something they had a lot of in the seminary. In fact they had more answers than there were questions. The sense was that everything had been decided and all we had to do was absorb it. Question a professor and you were out on the street. From September 1 to December 23, you did not leave the seminary grounds. Dentists, doctors, and bar-

15

bers were brought in. You could not call home or have family visits, even if the family lived a mile away. Still we knew we had it better than nuns. Nuns lost their names and were given new names, some of them pretty weird like Sister Matilda of the Holy Cross. Many nuns could not even get out to attend the funeral of a parent. We, at least, could do that and we had Christmas, Easter, and summer vacations. In some convents the mirrors in their baths were painted so they could not indulge in vanity, and in some, cloth binders were issued for their chests to flatten breast protuberances lest their endowments show. At least in the seminary nobody was worried about our chests. And our inevitable penile erections were a secret known only to God in his omniscient glory.

Surprises

"There are no experts on the future," as Israel's David Ben Gurion used to put it. After four years of study in Rome, I lay on the marble floor of the chapel in Rome and heard the bishop intone in Gregorian chant that I was now *sacerdos in aeternum,* "a priest forever." It was a dream fulfilled, and I cried to the surprise of my classmates. That moment should have marked the beginning of a quiet life in a little parish church. My view from the marble floor gave me no way of knowing the surprises of life that awaited. For example, how could I know . . .

◆ that *Ms. Magazine,* in its tenth anniversary issue in 1982, would list me, along with people like Phil Donahue and Alan Alda, as one of "40 male heroes of the last decade, men who took chances and made a difference."

◆ that Geraldine Ferraro would be denounced by New York's Cardinal O'Connor in the heat of her vice-presidential campaign for inviting me to do a briefing in Congress and then quoting me,

◆ that I would with Charles Curran lead a protest at The Catholic University of America in 1967 that would lead to a strike, shutting down the whole university, the only time in modern U.S. history,

◆ that I would be thrown out of that same university for committing matrimony and leaving the priesthood,

◆ that *Time Magazine* would write up my marriage under the title "End of a Battle,"

◆ that two FBI agents would come to my home in Milwaukee telling me a threat to the life of Justice Blackmun of the Supreme Court had been made and that it was signed "Dan Maguire, Marquette University," probably sent by The Army of God, a violent "pro-life" group, and they warned me to take special precautions for my life and that of my family,

◆ that 25 years after my ordination *People Magazine* would do an article entitled "Nine People the Pope Does Not Want To Meet On His Visit To the United States." And that I would be one of the nine,

◆ that *Time Magazine* would quote me on the election of Pope John Paul II as saying, I feared he would see the world as "Poland Writ Large" and that same pope would soon question my presence at Marquette University; but that Marquette (a Catholic Jesuit institution) would defend my academic freedom,

◆ that *The Milwaukee Journal* would then write a laudatory editorial entitled "Why Marquette Doesn't Muzzle Maguire,"

◆ that having earned the title "Father" as a priest, I would go on to earn that title in a second way, as the Daddy of two little boys, and that I would watch one of them slowly die of Hunter's Syndrome at age ten, and hear my 90-year-old Irish mother urging no extraordinary means, saying "let the poor wee man go to God."

◆ that I would meet Cardinal Ratzinger, now Pope Benedict XVI, in St. Peter's Piazza, and ask him if I could photograph him with my nine-year-old son. He granted the request with a smile, a smile that left when he heard who I was and he let me know he knew my work in theology and did not like it (that picture of him and my son smiles down on me now as I sit at my desk),

◆ that as president of the largest society of religious ethicists, The Society of Christian Ethics, I would tell my colleagues (among more abstruse things) that you can't do theology without babyshit in your fingernails,

◆ that I would have lunch at Drake University Law School with Clarence Thomas, then head of the EEOC, who was deeply offended by my talk on affirmative action—he a beneficiary of same—that he revealed himself in an interesting conversation that left me wondering "what plans do they have for this guy?"

◆ that I would publish thirteen books and 250 articles in scholarly journals and in *The New York Times* and that I would write a cover story for The Atlantic on "Death By Choice, Death By Chance,

◆ that I would be banned at most Catholic campuses as a speaker because of my pro-choice views on abortion, even though I am a tenured full professor at Marquette University, a Catholic Jesuit university, and that in March 2007, in a move the *New York Times* called "rare" and "unusual," the United States Catholic Conference of Bishops would call helpful attention to my work by denouncing it,

◆ that my great nephew, John Walker Lindh, would become a Muslim, go to Yemen and then join the Taliban, be denounced by John Ashcroft and now be serving a jail sentence of twenty years,

◆ that I would write in a book published by the State University of New York Press that "God" and "afterlife" beliefs are not facts but hypotheses that bear a high burden of proof,

◆ that I would for fourteen years be the president of The Religious Consultation on Population, Reproductive Health and Ethics (www.religiousconsultation.org) an international NGO of some 100 feminist, progressive, ecologically concerned, pro-choice international scholars funded by The Ford Foundation, The John D. and Catherine T. MacArthur Foundation, the David and Lucille

Packard Foundation, and The United Nations Fund for Population Activities, among others,

◆ that I would be given the opportunity to address the main assembly of delegates at the 1994 United Nations Conference on Population and Development in Cairo in 1994, with three delegates of "The Holy See" present, and criticize the Vatican for its misunderstandings of the richness of past Catholic teaching on issues such as contraception and abortion. My remarks were enthusiastically received except at the "The Holy See" desk from which there was stern glaring but no applause.

I never saw all that coming. How I dealt with it, sometimes well, sometimes anything but, is a story full of life with all its spices...and not a few lessons. I share it in these pages.

A Merry Memoir of Sex, Death, and Religion

CHAPTER TWO
THE LONG SHADOW OF AUGUSTINE'S PENIS

There we were. Fifty young men, ages 18 and 19, at the peak of our sexual potency, walking through that seminary door, committed to a sexless life forever and ever until death would us part from this earth. No questions asked. Not a one of us—and we were not the dumbest bunch of guys—not a one of us wondered why the church barred priests from all erotic joy. It was church law and the church represented God, and who was going to fight the Big Guy! We also never asked why the God that created the delights of sex didn't want us to have any of it.

It didn't occur to us that the Big Guy had nothing to do with it. Mainly, it was that wacky Augustine, the bishop who died in the year 430, who did us in. Augustine was a powerhouse writer, a booming intellect, whose Latin matched Cicero's in elegance. Nonetheless, he managed to spook the conscience of the West, and he is still at it. With all his smarts, Augustine was a loser when it came to sex. As much as anyone in the West, he was the one who made sex dirty. He was the one who convinced us young guys that in our entire lives, we must never fall in love.

Now of course odds-makers would say, put that plan up against the go-nads and the smart money will bet on the gonads every time. Sexuality is in us and a mighty force it is. The sex drive was around long before the church. Trying to suppress it by mandate is like trying to submerge an in-flated inner tube. Try as you might, some part of it will pop up. So to speak.

And speaking of popping up brings us back to Augustine and that pesky penis of his. In his youth he was a match for JFK in sexual energy. Even when he cooled down and stopped doing a lot of sex, he spent a lot of time writing about it. The problem was that when he got religion, he picked up a kind of sick form of it, infected by views that were very insulting to our sexuality. As a result, Augustine set out to make sure no one else ever had any sexual fun. His efforts to keep passion in exile were tortured and strained, and, made him become, well, downright silly.

If Augustine had been like most people who wrote in his times, his writ-ings would have been lost and we would never know about his anti-sex cru-sade. But, no. This fellow was out to be heard. He ordered multiple copies of his writings to be made to almost guarantee their survival. And survive they did. As a result, his penis cast a shadow over the next fifteen centuries. Now, let it be said, if you have an erection lasting more than fifteen centuries, see your doctor immediately. Augustine's shadow dominated a lot of church his-tory and lies behind the headlines modern priests have been making as their sexuality broke out negatively in the form of rape and abuse. It was there when the German Christian chaplains accompanying the army in its inva-sion of Holland in the Second World War were busily preaching sermons to the troops, warning them against the Dutch prostitutes. If it weren't for Au-gustine and his pals, they might have realized that it would have been better if the whole German army had stayed home and fornicated. But I digress.

When Theology Goes Silly

Let's get back to that beautiful sunny September day when we young men, hell-bent on celibacy, walked into that seminary. We did not even no-tice the shadow old Augustine was casting over us and the frustration he would cause us. Only later did we put Augustine and his neuroses on the couch to try to analyze how he got that way. Part of the answer is that he was the victim of shared ignorance. He and his contemporaries misunder-stood the first book of the Bible, the *Genesis* story of Adam and Eve and the Garden of Paradise. They thought it was history when actually, as modern scholars know, it was poetry.

The Genesis creation story was a poetic imagination of how life could be on this planet. This earth could be a paradise where we lived in harmony with one another and with the rest of nature. It was really brilliant stuff, but they didn't get it. Off scholars went for centuries looking for traces of the original Paradise, somewhere between the Tigris and the Euphrates, where life was perfect until Adam and Eve and the serpent blew the gig.

In that view, Paradise was the good old days, when life was perfect and everything was peachy between us and God. That in itself may have been a harmless mistake if Augustine hadn't dragged in his sicko idea that sex was dirty, defiling, base. In fact, it was so bad that Augustine cooked up an idea of "original sin," a spiritual blight that every child was born with. The new-born might have looked great but it was stained with sin and needed bap-tism in a hurry to clean up its act…even though it hadn't acted yet. No wonder people speak about ecclesiogenic psychoneurosis!

How did the poor little thing get that way? According to our man, it was the sexual passion that led to its conception that was so evil it contaminated the fetus leaving it in big time spiritual trouble. (I was rushed off to church the day after I was born lest I die and be denied heaven because of that "original sin" thing.) Had Augustine heard of cloning, he would have loved it. The baby would arrive clean as a whistle, untouched by the infectious horror of sexual joy.

Sex in Paradise

There were problems in Augustine's fictive paradise. People lived in Paradise and they needed sex to reproduce. Fine, said Augustine, there was sex in Paradise, but there was no sexual pleasure. Why no pleasure? Because it was the pleasure that was sinful and bad. Sex without pleasure would not be a problem. I'm happy to report that some of his hearers with a practical bent of mind saw a problem there. They wondered just how the men of Paradise would get it up to do their reproductive chore without any sexual pleasure. Remember, these were pre-Viagra times. Their question was a commonsensical question, proving there was common sense back then, even if Augustine didn't have much of it.

Questions demand answers and Augustine was nothing if not an answer man. His answer was a whopper.

Augustine assured his people that the merry men of paradise would get it up by sheer will power, without the slightest taint of fun. They just could simply will it up. I am relieved to report that continued skepticism greeted this reply. The folks could not grasp the idea of intercourse without pleasure.

Poor Augustine. Back to the drawing boards he went to prove his fun-free sex theory. His next answer makes one wonder what sort of parties he used to go to. Will power, he insisted, could do wonders. Why he had seen people, even now in our fallen, sin-battered, post-paradisiacal state who by a simple act of will could wiggle an ear. More convincing yet, he added, he had seen some truly gifted persons who could actually wiggle both ears at the same time using their sin-broken wills to do it.

The ear-wiggling should have clinched it. If the broken, sin-battered will could wiggle both ears surely the perfect will in Paradise could pop a penis. How could the people get around that one!

It is again reassuring to hear that some of his skeptical hearers still didn't buy it.

Back to his desk went the brave Augustine. He needed more feats of will power, and he found one. With his back against the wall, his attention turned to flatulence. Here was his *piece de resistence*. "Some can produce at will odorless sounds from their breech, a kind of singing from the other end." Surely then the people of Paradise could make sexual music without enjoying it.

In Fairness to Poor Old Augustine

In a display of fairness I should say that Augustine did not have only bad ideas. He taught that a state which does not practice justice is nothing more than organized crime. That has lots of contemporary application. He also held that the early fetus had the moral status of a plant. When it developed further, it had the moral standing of an animal. Only when it was fully formed did it merit the name of "baby." Without the benefit of advanced embryology he was ahead of those today who would call fertilized eggs "people," you know, citizens like you and me. Thomas Aquinas, by the way, agreed with Augustine. Early fetuses are not people, the implication being that abortion of such fetuses is not murder. Sorry "pro-lifers," a lot of your heroes are not on your side, proving again the old axiom that conservatives are the worshipers of dead liberals.

Augustine was asked whether unformed early fetuses would rise in the final resurrection of the dead at the end of history, an event anticipated in those days. Quite consistently, he replied in the negative. Early fetuses would not rise with fully born persons on that happy day. If he had stopped there it would have been better for him but he sallied on. It wasn't until the nineteenth century that the human egg was discovered by science. Prior to that it was thought that the sperm was the whole show, each sperm being in miniature an itsy-bitsy baby needing only the oven of a woman's womb to grow up. So on the final resurrection of the dead at the climax of history,

Augustine was asked if all the sperm of history would arise on that grand day of glory. Augustine said they would not. What a relief! Think of the mess it would have been with all the saints slipping and sliding on that stuff as history reached its glorious finale.

Augustine's Children

Augustine's sexophobia did not die with him; it spawned a pandemic in Christian history. It filled the seminary through whose portals we passed. Through most of that history, sexual pleasure, even in marriage, was thought to be sinful. Gregory the Great put it bluntly: "Pleasure can never be without sin." There's a jolly thought for you. And the rule was, the more pleasure, the more sin. William of Auxerre in the thirteenth century said that a holy man who has sex with his wife and finds it hateful and disgusting commits no sin. He added, with poignant regret (and a bit of insight) that this, however, "seldom happens."

The twelfth century Petrus Cantor opined that sex with a beautiful woman was a greater sin since it caused greater delight. It's a relief to know that his point was debated... but not much of a relief. His contemporary Alain de Lille demurred, saying sex with a beautiful woman was less sinful because the man was "compelled by the sight of her beauty, and "where the compulsion is greater, the sin is slighter." (Taken to its logical extreme, this would justify the rape of overwhelmingly beautiful women.)

Albert, who was called The Great, was not great on sex. He labeled it an "evil," a "punishment," "filthy," "defiling," "ugly," "shameful," "sick," a "degradation of the mind," a "humiliation of reason by the flesh," "debasing," "humiliating," "shared with the beasts," "brutal," "corrupted," "depraved," "infected and infecting." You get the idea. He urged thirty nights of chastity for newlyweds. Lots of luck on that one!

26

Albert had stories to back up his theories of sex as blight. One story had a kind of *Schadenfreude* about it. It seems that a monk in Bohemia, a man already graying, was consumed with lust for a beautiful woman. Finally he had his way with her for a full night. According to Albert, the man was a veritable prodigy, one for the Guinness Book of Records. In that one night, "up until the ringing of matins," he had sex with that woman sixty-six times. In the morning, they found him dead. No surprise. (There is no mention as to whether he had a smile on his face.) Because he was a nobleman, his body was opened up and it was found that his brain had drained and shrunken to the size of a pomegranate. His eyes were as good as destroyed. Albert has no reports on the condition of the poor woman who participated in this sexual tsunami.

Albert also said too much sex leads to baldness. Bad enough you lose your hair; you lose your reputation too. And on top of that, Albert noticed that people who have a lot of sex have a cadaverous smell and are often followed around by dogs. So if you see a lot of dogs following after a bald man, you know what that rascal is up to.

Thomas Aquinas reached the conclusion that loving one's wife too ardently is worse than adultery. Wouldn't that have prompted some guys to say: "OK, if adultery is less sinful, I'll stick to that."

Science Can be Dumb Too

Don't think that religiosees are the only ones who get goofy on sex. Christianity need not shoulder all the blame for Western sexual neurosis. Science chipped in. The first psychiatry textbook published in the United States said that masturbation "produces seminal weakness, impotence, dysury, tabes dorsalis, pulmonary consumption, dyspepsia, dimness of sight, vertigo, epilepsy, hypochondriasis, loss of memory, manalgia, fatuity and death." Other experts thought this listing incomplete and added that it caused senility, stupidity, melancholy, homosexuality, suicide, hysteria, mania, religious delusions, auditory hallucination, conceit, defective offspring, and eventually racial decay. The masturbator, it was said, is incapable "of any generous impulse or act of loyalty; he is dead to the call of his family, his country, or of humanity."

How many gentle masturbators reading this would like to plead guilty to those charges?

Back to Chastity Central

Now let's get back to me at the seminary gate, caught in the rip tide of all of this. The Catholic Church had decided, drinking from these poisoned wells, that only celibate hands can touch the sacraments. Only candidates with subdued penises should ascend the altar steps. (Since we have no idea if Jesus himself was married or not, it was indeed a curious requirement. Isn't it interesting how most Christians assume Jesus had no sex life... and how revealing of their negative view of sex!) Sex in the seminary, and in convents, was viewed as a demonic force crouching in the wings, ever on the ready to intrude.

Yes, Homophobia Too

The seminary was a girl-free zone, making it easier on us heterosexuals. There was, however, a heap of homophobia onboard. From day one, we were warned against "particular friendships," a term so prominent in seminary discipline that commonly only the initials were used, PF. No seminarian should spend too much time with another seminarian. That would be a PF and very suspect. At the first drumming home of this message, a fellow first-year candidate (who bailed out within months) commented to me: "What do they think we are, a pack of queers?" In spite of all this neurotic screening and surveillance, quite a few gays slipped through and got ordained, as we now know.

When I was on the faculty at St. Mary's Seminary in Baltimore some years later, we would have regular faculty discussions about the seminarians, bringing up things about the candidates that looked good or not so good. I was the youngster at the table for these discussions. I heard some of the older Sulpician Fathers using a term I did not understand. I could tell it was good—it was what you ought to be—but I did not get its meaning. I decided I'd best wait and figure it out from its usage. The term was "angular." Angular was good, very good. Thus a seminarian might be praised by one of the older Fathers as "a good student, obedient, pleasant, prayerful, and angular." There it was. What did it mean? It made me wonder quietly whether I myself was angular.

Eventually I figured it out. Angular was the polite form of macho. It was the antonym of effeminate. An angular student was out kicking footballs and roughing it up with the guys. No flaccid handshakes from these angular fellows. Effeminate students would often be told without explanation that they did not "have a vocation" and were dismissed. The myth that all gays are effeminate and all non-effeminate men are heterosexual was the ruling assumption. Of course, this conceptual hole in the fence let a lot of gay students get through...all the way to ordination.

Keeping It Down

So sexual pleasure was the banned bugaboo, and yet its excommunication was not without tension. There was a foreboding sense that the allures of sex were always threateningly close. Things were even more neurotic at one of the Roman seminaries. Bishop Carroll McCormick who studied at the Lateran Seminary in Rome told me that they were given paddles to tuck in their shirts, lest their hands start roaming down there and move from tuck to forbidden touch. He also said the showers, which were permitted on only a weekly basis had wire meshing over each of the cubicles, lest perhaps a student might be tempted to climb over to consort with another naked student. Keeping that inner tube submerged was a full time job.

Of course, women did sneak into the seminaries, but not by way of medieval monastic tunnels. They rode in on the Bible where healthier views of sexual joy could not be expunged.

Small wonder that some religious orders blacked out certain lusty texts of the Bible as not conducive to celibacy training.

The Song of Songs is an exuberant celebration of erotic lovemaking. The man says to his lover (there is no hint as to whether the lovers are married!): "How beautiful you are, my dearest, how beautiful! Your eyes...Your hair...Your teeth...Your lips...Your parted lips...Your words...Your neck...Your two breasts.. You are beautiful, my dearest, beautiful without a flaw."

The woman in turn gives a lush description of her lover, missing not a detail; she revels in it all, "his head....his eyes...his cheeks...his lips...his arms...his body...his legs...his appearance...his speech..." Having fixed her hot gaze on all of that, her response is not a surprise: "I have stripped off my dress...When my beloved slipped his hand through the latch-hole, my bowels stirred within me. When I arose to open for my beloved, my hands dripped with myrrh..." He thrills at the sight of her: "How beautiful, how entrancing you are, my loved one, daughter of delights! You are stately as a palm tree, and your breasts are the clusters of dates...I will climb up into the palm to grasp its fronds. May I find your breasts like clusters of grapes on the vine, the scent of your breath like apricots, and your whispers like spiced wine, flowing smoothly to welcome my caresses, gliding down through lips and teeth." (*The New English Bible*)

Give me a break! How were we poor celibates-in-training supposed to deal with that drippingly sexual feast—and all of it described in the book that was called "the inspired word of God"! And it wasn't just the Song of Songs. I remember reading the psalms on the beach on summer vacation and there was the psalmist thanking and praising God for their young women who were as lovely as "carved columns." And there was I being driven nuts by the bikini-ed carved columns that were walking by and I wasn't thanking God for them like the psalmist, because I wasn't allowed to get near one. It was not a prayerful experience.

Scholarship eventually came to our aid. As Bible scholar Walter Wink writes: "The Old Testament regarded celibacy as abnormal, and 1 Tim. 4:1-2 calls compulsory celibacy a heresy." No wonder this juridically imposed, not at all job-related celibacy thing is more and more perceived as a foreign object, and suffering the fate that foreign objects suffer in healthy bodies.

The Napoleonic Code

The jurisprudential atmosphere in the seminary was Napoleonic: you were presumed guilty and unworthy of the priesthood until you were proven innocent by continuous scrutiny and finally ordained. We were reminded of all those who wanted to get in the seminary and did not make it. All of them were out there waiting to take our place. After four years, chock full of Latin and Greek Studies, the school year at St. Charles Seminary, Overbrook ended as always with a solemn ceremony in the chapel, called the *Concursus.* Right before we were to go there, I was summoned to the Rector's office. I was terrified. I knew there were only two possibilities: either I was being told I did not " have a vocation" and would be dismissed, or I had been chosen to complete my studies in Rome at the Pontifical North American College, a great honor. I had no idea which it was, dismissal or honor. That's how well they resisted "positive reinforcement." The rector, Monsignor Francis Furey laughingly told someone later how scared and blanched I looked when I ventured into his office. (Fun stuff!) Even when he told me the honorific news, there was a bit of a stick in it. "You have done well in your studies here. We expect you to do even better next year in Rome."

I was excited by the news and I should not have been. We were taught to receive honors humbly and almost unwillingly. *Quamquam invitus*, although unwilling, was the way saints accepted honors, or so we were told.

Not me. Four years in Europe, internationally known professors; it was a deal and a half and I knew it and I quietly exulted. A stumbling start into sainthood to be sure.

When I brought the news home, my mother was out doing her work as a seamstress, and my easygoing father was home, "in between jobs" as later jargon would have it. He knew being sent to Rome was an honor but he also knew I would not be home for vacations for those four years. When my mother got home he announced: "There's news, and it's both good news and bad news." My mother's reply: "You got a job?" "No, Danny's being sent to Rome."

CHAPTER THREE
VIVA L'ITALIA!!

It was a beautiful September day in New York when I stepped onto the impressive USS Independence bound for Rome. Ships were such a civilized way to cross the ocean. "Modern" is not always progress. On board an ocean liner, you weren't crammed like anchovies into the entrails of an airplane, stuck in seats designed for midgets. To make things worse, for no good reason, the plane takes off in the evening from New York and dumps you in a bedraggled condition after a fitful hour or two of sleep, into Europe where everyone is in a morning mood, refreshed and perky and ready for a new day.

Shipboard life was exhilarating. Breathing the ocean air, strolling the lovely decks, enjoying afternoon tea served to you on your deck chair. You arrived with more energy than you had on embarking. That was the way it was before air travel encroached, all in the name of Speed, the enslaving god of our modernity.

The dock on the day of a sailing was full of festive excitement, packed with well-wishers seeing the travelers off. Non-passengers could come aboard and party a while until the deep horn sounded and they were ordered ashore.

"All ashore that are going ashore!"Then we on board would throw balls of paper ribbon down toward them so that we could hold one end of it while they held the other, til the link broke as the ship inched out of dockage.

The Archdiocese of Philadelphia sent me first class, which was a waste. The food was too fancy and beyond the customs of my palate. Four years of seminary cooking was not a crash course on gourmet food. And before that my mother was one terrible cook. She was a master seamstress, a great conversationalist and a woman who insisted, along with my father, that in our house humor always had the right of way. All that was great, but, as a cook she was awful. We used to joke that if you wanted a good meal, go home to mom, and take her out to dinner. I had never known meat that was not burnt. My mother came from an Ireland where refrigeration was not available and so her maxim was "you have to cook the badness out of meat." And with the badness went the goodness.

A sophisticated lady who was at my first class table on the ship shocked me no end when the waiter asked how she wanted her steak done. She replied with a sweet southern drawl: "Just knock the horns off and warm it up a little." It arrived swimming in its own blood, and she actually ate it! Meanwhile, I was thinking: I wish they served hamburgers…well done.

My family and many classmates from the Philadelphia seminary I was now leaving came to see me off. I was excited. I was also scared. I was heading off for years of study at the Gregorian University where my classmates and professors would come from all over the world. The *lingua franca* used to teach us would be Latin. Everything in Latin. The lectures, the text books, the exams. This was right out of the Middle Ages. Even if the professor examining you in an oral exam was an American you both had to talk Latin. I had eight years of Latin and four years of Greek so I was better off than many of those seminarians on board from other dioceses in the U.S. who were still almost at the *amo, amas, amat* stage. Some did not survive. But it was still daunting for me too. And thrilling.

34

The Great Irony

What was the reason for sending American seminarians off to Rome to study theology when theology was taught right in their own seminary at home? The one word answer is Romanity, or *romanitas* as they Latin-ed it. We would be studying in a Vatican-monitored university. We would be molded into a Vatican orthodoxy mindset and then we could come home and help to Vaticanize the American church. That was the plan. As often is the fate of "best laid plans," they forgot something. They forgot the Italians. Big, big mistake.

The professors at the Gregorian University worked hard to teach me. And so did the Italians, and these two schools of thought were not in sync. I got my first lesson in a restaurant shortly after my arrival. I had an inkling even before I got there…from knowing Italian Americans…that there was a somewhat different brand of Catholicism over there.

I arrived in a restaurant on a Friday evening. I had checked upon arrival in Rome what the *Ordo*, the official rule book of the Roman church, had to say about abstinence from meat on Fridays. The *Ordo* could not have been clearer. No meat on a Friday anywhere in Italy, and they added, the same rule applied also *in insulis adiacentibus*, in all the adjacent islands. No slipping over to Capri or Sicily to feast on steak on a Friday. That was reassuring to me, an Irish American who was taught to take such stuff seriously. Hey, I even knew that you could not even fry an egg on Friday in bacon grease, much less eat the bacon. So I was chock full of orthodoxy when I sat at the restaurant table.

Meatless in Rome?

I searched the menu looking for a meatless pasta. Not a one in sight! Everything had a meat component or sauce. This was vexing. Here I was in Rome, the center of the church and I could not find a meatless meal on a Friday. I called over the waiter and pointed out the problem, which, in a Catholic country, one should not have to point out. The waiter gave me a look that seemed to say: "Why do I always end up with nuts like this?" I chose to ignore that look and pressed on.

He politely joined me in the search for a meatless item on the menu. He offered a few examples, but then had to back off saying *c'e carne*, there's meat in there. Finally, with a sigh of relief, he found something. A pasta stuffed with spinach! "*Finalmente*," I said with more than a bit of irritation.

I ordered a glass of wine and sat awaiting my meatless pasta. Then, my spinach stuffed pasta arrived…gloriously and copiously topped with *Bolognese* meat sauce. I was outraged. I rebuked the waiter, asking him: "*Cattolico, lei?*" *(Aren't you a Catholic?)* His answer put me away, and even without a lesson in Italian you can translate it: "Cattolico, si; fanatico, no," I'm a Catholic but not a fanatic.

Guess what? I ate the pasta, meat and all and I didn't choke to death. I did order another glass of wine to help my troubled conscience, but somehow the waiter had gotten through to me. Something inside me knew that Jesus had never said, "By this shall they know that you are my disciples, that you don't eat meat on Fridays." Search the gospels; it's not there. The gospels were not into diet. They were into heavy duty stuff like justice and compassion and the futility of violence.

Back to the Books

I was still a little uneasy, so after dinner, off I went to the Gregorian University library. I sought out an Italian moral theology textbook, written in Italian for Italians. I made my way to the section on fasting and abstinence. Surprise. There were all the strict rules spelled out in detail. However, and here is where the plot thickened, or should I say, thinned…the rules were followed by three pages of excusing causes that freed you from having to pay the least bit of attention to all those rules just spelled out in full rigor. The list of the excused included *operaii*, laborers, and the family of the laborer. Also excused from all fasting and abstinence were the ill, the convalescing, pregnant or nursing women, teachers of children, and health care givers. The list went on and on. It would be impossible not to qualify on at least a half a dozen counts.

The Italian message was: here are the rules and these rules are very strict. Now forget about them. There is more important stuff in life. And to think the Vatican City State was just a few blocks away and this book was housed in this "Pontifical" library, one specially authorized by the Vatican itself. Something was not adding up, but my education was on its way, strangely set on two separate tracks that rarely seemed to cross.

The Vatican Monsignor

In a tribute to my doggedly Irish Catholic training, not even the Italian moral theology book satisfied me. I needed to hear from a live voice, an authoritative voice. So I phoned the Vicariate, the headquarters of the diocese of Rome. It could not get more official than this. I polished up my Italian as best I could so that I could make my case. I got a monsignor on the phone. I pointed out that I had read the dietary rules in the official *Ordo* and I wondered if they were still in force. The first reply I got was a groan. It seemed to say "why did I pick up that phone?" This was not encouraging, and it reminded me a lot of the Italian waiter, but I had no choice but to keep at it. This was my last best chance to get a definitive answer.

I narrowed down my question to Lent, when lots of fasting and abstinence was demanded by the published rules. "Do we or do we not have to fast and abstain during Lent?" There was a sigh and a pause at the other end of the line and then came this mystifying answer: "No you don't have to fast and abstain during Lent, except, maybe on Good Friday." What leapt out

at me was that "maybe" so I jumped on it. "Do we really have to fast and abstain on Good Friday?" The answer was a little slow in coming, but it ended
the conversation: "No, and good bye." Somehow these Italians seemed to
know that whatever Jesus was up to, dietary planning was not his mission.
Also, war had passed through Italy many times and getting food was the
concern, not setting up arbitrary restrictions on eating it.

The Orgasmic Wife

The North American College was our residence while we attended the
Gregorian University. It was a grand building perched on the Janiculum
Hill overlooking Rome and the Vatican. We studied hard and ate poorly.
This was, after all, the training ground for prospective bishops. Not all of us
would be bishops—I, for example, due to a few slip-ups never made it—but
when bishops were chosen they were most likely from the North American College. Many even made it as Cardinals. If we behaved, we could at
least expect to become monsignors. (I didn't even make that.)

The college brochures advertised that we got bacon and eggs for breakfast. They did not say that on one day we would get one hard-boiled egg and
on the next day one piece of bacon to go with some bread. The theory
seemed to be that, as in residency programs for doctors, because you were
destined for great things, you had to pay a stiff price in training.

When the price took a toll on our health, we were allowed to go off for a
week of recovery. Our favorite retreat was to the Irish "Blue Nuns" who ran a
guest house in Fiesole, called the Villa San Gerolomo. A lovely place it was,
set on a mountain side, looking down on the Arno river valley winding its way
through Florence in the distance below. Fiesole is rich in history, from Etruscan
ruins to decayed Roman fortifications. It was said to be the mountain on which
Leonardo da Vinci tested the principle of flight. The Villa San Gerolomo got
its name from the fact that in the past it had been the headquarters of a religious order known as the Gerolomiti. Sadly, the Gerolomiti lapsed from virtue

in a rather big way, and, as the story went, got into some hefty debauchery. Hey, nobody's perfect! However somebody snitched and the Vatican found out about the shameful doings at the Villa San Gerolomo.

When the messenger from the Vatican came with the writ announcing to these jolly monks that they had been suppressed as a religious order and should disband immediately, the poor messenger was not well received. He interrupted a boisterous banquet, and, sad to tell, the drunken monks tore into the poor fellow, and killed him. Still, the suppression stuck and the Gerolomiti were toast.

So the lovely villa in Fiesole was drenched in history, not all of it edifying. At any rate, the Irish nuns were edifying and they fattened us for a week before returning us to boot camp.

On one of those salvific visits to Fiesole, a seminarian friend and I were strolling in the gardens of the villa. We were dressed in our black cassocks, looking very much the ecclesiastics we were. Some Italian visitors were there and one of the men came over to chat with us. The Italians didn't have the highest esteem for ecclesiastics but on the one-to-one level they were always courteous. (In Rome where there were so many of us clerics teeming around the streets in our black robes, they called us *Bacherozzi*, cockroaches. The alumni of the North American College still call themselves "Bags," derived from that uncomplimentary title the Romans gave us.)

The man who joined us regaled us with stories about Florence and Fiesole and it was a thoroughly delightful time, until, of a sudden, he almost shocked the Roman collars off our necks. His wife was nearby chatting with some other guests. At one point she was admiring the tall and lovely cypress trees for which Italy is famous. Suddenly, carried away with the beauty of it all, she threw up her arms and shouted loudly *"Queste magnifiche cypressse!!"* (*These magnificent cypresses!*) Her husband looked at her with a warm and approving smile and commented: "*Mia moglie e piena di orgasmo!!*" *(My wife is full of orgasm!)* We two ecclesiastics knew that *orgasmo* was the Italian word for sexual climax...and our pious jaws collapsed.

It took me years to realize the lesson taught in that garden. The Italians were so at home with their sexuality that they could use the word orgasm metaphorically without raising a single Italian eyebrow. My seminarian friend and I were double-whammied by our sexually skittish Irish American culture and by the church's gloomy uneasiness with sexual pleasure...and we, of course, were in training for a life devoid of sexual pleasure! (I'm glad that didn't work out for either one of us.)

Only later could I realize how perfect was the Italian husband's description of his enthusiastic, dynamic, and fully alive wife. His comment perfectly captured her vivacious and ecstatic responsiveness to beauty. Frigidity in the face of beauty is a curse and this woman had none of it. (My wife and I to this day use the phrase *piena di orgasmo* to describe friends and people we meet whose spirited response to the good of life requires no lesser encomium.)

Train Lessons

Italian trains are among the friendliest places on earth. People chat and offer to share food and wine with you. On this particular day, I would have none of that. I had no time for Italian friendliness. I had to study...probably studying something that was considerably less wise than my fellow travelers. I was sitting in those little ten-seat compartments on an Italian train. I chose it because this one was empty. Soon, however, a man entered and later a woman. I decided to pretend I knew no Italian so I could be alone with my books.

The two began to talk. First of all about me. They remarked with hedged admiration that it was nice to see a young man so "*studioso,*" so wrapped up in his books. But then, with more enthusiasm, they went on to say how much nicer it was to sit and have "*una bella conversazione.*" After that, they ignored me and turned to more interesting subjects.

First up, the cost of living. Prices were high, wages, low, that sort of thing. I paid little heed. But then, talk of finances led to family planning, a veritable Catholic obsession. Suddenly my young orthodox Catholic ears perked up. The man said he had a family of three children and a moderate salary so he and his wife used birth control so as not to have any more. I wasn't pleased. There was no effort to justify himself. He knew the church teaching but he simply did not find it applicable to his circumstances. He wasn't angry at the teaching…just calmly and confidently dismissive. He even remarked that "the bishops and the pope" have problems with contraception, but he added confidently in his own defense, "I know, however, that I am a good Christian!" (*So bene pero che sono un bon Cristiano!*) The situation became even more scandalous and offensive to my pious ears as the woman gave her unfledging support to his heretical theological judgment.

"These Italians!" I disdainfully thought. I was still a seminarian, not yet a priest, and it struck me again with force, that if, when I returned to Philadelphia as a priest and got stationed in an Italian American parish, I would have my work cut out for me. These people just did not get it. At least they did not get it the way the pope got it—and we Irish got it—and it was somehow obvious to me then that on sexual and other matters, the celibate pope knew best.

Now some of the pope's historical predecessors might have been in a better position to offer judgments on sex. I refer to those medieval popes who used to throw bacchanalian sex parties in the Lateran Palace on a regular basis, keeping the local prostitutes in business. The most that could be said of them was they seemed to have avoided contraception since they sired a lot of bastards, some of whom they later, with parental pride, appointed to high positions in the church. Those dudes could talk sex with some authority but Pope Pius XII did not appear to be a rake. Italians had no trouble blowing off his teaching on sex. As one man on a bus said to me in his broken English, "if he no play the game, he no make the rules." Fair enough.

A Happy Priestly Family

"Scattershot" would describe how the Italian shocks came to us, when we were least expecting them. One of our classmates, an Italian American named Armando went down to Bari in southern Italy to visit relatives he had never met. They lived in a lovely little town up in the mountains. Armando was received with great warmth and there was much feasting for the *cugino Americano*. Being a good seminarian, Armando went to church every morning. There he met the pastor, a charming man who was delighted to invite Armando into the rectory where he lived for *caffè* after Mass each morning. That is where the shock occurred.

The pastor was not lonely. There was a lovely woman there, strangely referred to as Maria Prete. Maria is fine, but *prete* means priest. And that was not all. There were five children living in the priest house all with the same priestly suffix added to their name: Benedetto Prete, Giovanni Prete, Susanna Prete and a two-year-old Maria Prete. Give this pastor credit. He was not defying the church by practicing birth control but he had quite nicely dispensed himself from that unpleasant celibacy requirement.

What made this worse (or better) was that the whole village knew this and had no problem with it. Probably the men were happy that this attractive man had his own woman, his own sex life, and they didn't have to worry when they were away at market. Whatever! The villagers all found it perfectly fine. Celibacy did not strike Italians as a sensible idea. *Viva l'amore!* was part of the Italian soul. Later when I was a priest in an Italian parish in Philadelphia I had helped a couple who felt close to me, close enough to ask me one time "where do priests go for sex?" Attractive as the idea was, I appropriately corrected them and gave them my celibacy defense spiel. I wasn't sure they bought it, especially when I heard the man quoted later as saying, "I can't believe that priest doesn't have a chick on the side." These Italians!

Of course, my later studies pointed out that scholars are divided on whether Jesus was married. Some say he definitely was married since the social pressure to be married was enormous at that time and he could not escape it without seeming an anomaly. Others say he was too busy defying the Roman occupation and the corrupt Jewish leaders to have time. Bottom line; nobody knows. We do know that Peter, often presented as the first pope was married. There is reference to his "mother in law" in the gospel. Not a bad model for the modern popes. Papal wives could be great teachers. The odds are there never would have been an encyclical banning contraceptives if the pope had a wife. She would have said, "if you issue this silly thing I'm moving to a separate bedroom!" And papal children could also be great teachers. A pope raising teenagers would learn a lot about life.

The Pious Cab Driver

In 1968, Pope Paul VI, who, I am sorry to say, was not married, issued his misguided encyclical banning all contraceptives…except of course Vatican Roulette, as some people call the " rhythm method," or "natural family planning" method where you try to guess when the woman is fertile. Problem: you never know if that gun is loaded or if some hungry little egg will manage a tryst with one of those spermy little swimmers. Anyhow, the pope set his target on condoms, pills and diaphragms and blasted away on an August day in 1968. He called his encyclical *Humanae Vitae,* On Human Life. A story that came out of Rome at that time confirmed all the little lessons I had learned as a student in Rome on what Italians thought Catholicism ought to be.

Huge excitement greeted the encyclical when it came out. Liberal theologians had been predicting a change in the ban on contraception; conservatives had been saying No Way, and the conservatives won. The new media were ablaze with the story of the papal crackdown.

A cab driver was doing the Vatican beat that day and every passenger he picked up was talking about the encyclical. Finally, he picked up a priest and decided to check it out. *"Scusi, Padre, ma cos' e sucesso?"(Pardon me Father what happened?)* The priest replied solemnly: "The Holy Father came out today and condemned the contraceptive pill." The cabby moaned at this news, shook his head sadly and asked: "Why did they tell him about it?"

That simple question spoke volumes about Italian Catholicism. The cabby was a Catholic. He liked the pope. It was just that the pope was not pope-ing well that day, and the cabby put the blame smack on his advisors. Why were they bothering that old man about stuff like birth control? He seemed to assume the pope would not have heard about stuff like this unless some finicky Monsignor in the Vatican went up to him and said: "Holy Father do you know what they are doing now?" Then the conservatives in the Vatican wrote that nasty encyclical and got him to sign it.

Clearly the encyclical would not make the slightest difference in the behavior of this Catholic cabby. The entire issue was reduced to a case of stupid advisors. *"Povero Papa!"* (the poor pope) the priest could hear the cabby muttering as he drove through Rome's busy streets. The pope wanted compliance; all he got from this Italian Catholic was pity.

CHAPTER FOUR
BREAKING FREE

I f the seminary was a girl-free zone, the world we entered as young priests was not. We picked up on that right away. We did not arrive hormone-free. We noticed women—we really did—and we noticed to our surprise that women noticed us. Apparently they have hormones too. The celibacy discipline ran smack into life. We newly minted priests were a fledgling flock of innocents. We came out thinking that all was as we had been trained to think it ought to be. We also came out thinking we too were just what we were supposed to be. Human nature would not get in the way of our training.

It was all so confusing. The God Eros seemed to be at odds with the Catholic God. Their divine agendas were on a collision course. And that brings me to

The Gentleness of Wisdom

When I was newly ordained, I was sent to a delightful Italian parish in Philadelphia. There I had a wise, witty, and wonderful old Italian pastor, a native of Piemonte. His portrait still hangs in my home and memories of his wisdom still warm my mind. A lot of priests would not hang a portrait of their pastors; being more inclined, perhaps, to hang the pastor but I lucked out. My first appointment was to an Italian parish, Our Lady of Loreto in southwestern Philadelphia. I arrived there more aware of what I needed to teach these people than of what these people were about to teach me. After all, it was well known in the Archdiocese that many Italians came to church only three times a year: Christmas, Easter and Palm Sunday. Using the Italian names for those three days we called them, derisively, the *Natalini, Pasqualini,* and *Palmini.* Obviously I had to change all that and get them running to church every Sunday like the Irish—the real Catholics—did.

The pastor was a sweet man full of Italian good sense, an Italian look-alike of Barry Fitzgerald, with white hair, a soft voice, and an embracing smile. Giovanni Matteo Amateis was his name. He was one of the kindest persons I ever knew: gentle, good humored, realistic about human weakness, but always full of hope. I used to say that he greeted every morning the way kids greet Christmas, with expectation of wondrous things to come. His antennae were set to the positive and that brought a lot of positives his way.

However, there was a problem, and my Irish eyes spotted it right away. Many of the men in the parish, reflecting customs from the old country, never darkened the door of the church. It was mostly women who filled the pews. Worse yet, some of these men would drive their wives to church, and then, to pass the time while their wives were in church, would come over to the rectory to visit with Fr. Amateis whom they all loved and revered. Worse yet, Fr. Amateis would receive them and offer them coffee or *un bicchiere di vino.*

This was heavy duty trouble, and I was obviously the man to attend to it. Not only were these men missing Mass, which was classified as "mortal sin," but the saintly pastor was entertaining them as they did so. After a while, I could bear this scandal no longer and I spoke to Fr. Amateis. He listened calmly to my concerns, and just as calmly blew them off with a sim-

ple "Don't worry. These are good people, very good people.' (*Non ti preoc-
cupi. Son' buoni, son'buoni!*)

Only slowly did it dawn on me that religion has no good purpose but
to make people good, and if it doesn't do that, it is worse than worthless. He
was telling me these men were good. The *end* was being achieved and I was
quibbling about the *means*. In a year or so, as the wisdom of this old man
seeped in, I began to sit in on the visits of these non-church-attending hus-
bands, and share a coffee with them. And Fr. Amateis was right. They were
good. One of them heard once that Fr. Amateis, who was near eighty,
tripped slightly on a loose rug near the altar. Immediately the man, at his
own expense, had the rugs around the altar replaced and installed in a way
that would be safe. Yes, I finally agreed, *son' buoni, son' buoni!*"

The Housekeeper's Tale

The housekeeper, an elderly Italian woman, was another bit of luck.
She was wise and very bright, and she knew priests…did she ever know
priests!! She had decades of parish experience. When I had been there about
a month, she sat down with me as I lunched one day to give me a lesson she
had obviously given many times before, with uneven success. She sat across
from me at the table with a serious magisterial sort of look. I knew I was in
for some kind of a lecture.

Italians, of course, are masters of gestures as well as of words and she
began with a dramatic gesture. Saying nothing, she rolled up her sleeve, and
slapped her arm a couple of times dramatically. Very Italian. No wonder
those people are good at opera.

Next came the words, the aria, and the words were a firestorm of logic.
"Father Maguire," she began still tapping her arm "the priest has the red
blood just like everyone else and just because the priest say the Mass does-

n't mean he no need the woman!" Wow! Mass and woman in the same sentence! And her point was clear. A gesture and just a few words made it blunt and clear. Because you have one thing doesn't mean you don't need the other. That was too much. All my training was being offended.

I was shocked, and being a proper priest, I protested. I told her how we took a solemn promise of celibacy when we were ordained subdeacons, repeated it as deacons, and swore to it upon ordination to the priesthood. After a polite moment of silence, her response was a simple, emphatic, "No!"

She then went on to file a brief, a detailed brief, chock full of facts about the sexual doings of priests that she had seen in her fifty years of parish work. It was a chilling performance, giving names and circumstances in which these un-celibate deeds were done. Since I was to be living under this woman's trained eye, it was fair warning that I had better behave myself.

The housekeeper's lesson, however, had just begun. And she had my full attention. She went on to tell me there were three kinds of priests and she was recommending I fit into tier two. Tier one was for priests like the saintly pastor. His heroic sanctity was marked by two features: he never ran around with women, and, he was always patient with the housekeeper when meals did not arrive on time, which in this rectory they never did. She was presenting him as the unusual supererogatory and charismatic model and she would not require that from me. You can't demand heroism.

The bottom tier of priests that she wanted me to avoid had two markers: these rascals hit on women in the parish and were, to top it off, impatient with the housekeeper. It seems that the two failings were part of the same syndrome. She cited no cases where a priest was impatient with the housekeeper and also chaste, or where a sexually rambunctious priest was nevertheless patient with the housekeepers. With prosecutorial zeal, she started ticking off the names of a few of these bottom tier priests.

There were narratives to go with the names. "Father X," she told me, "fell in love with a good looking woman on Waltham Avenue." Waltham Avenue was right at the edge of the parish, but still within the parish. "Waltham Avenue," she said, pounding on the table, "is too close, much too close." I took it that if I operated just a bit beyond Waltham Avenue, I was considered to be in a free zone.

The recommended goal for me was tier two: these priests were always patient with the housekeeper, never grousing about meal times. However, and my jaw kept dropping, these tier two priests did not have to be chaste. There was sexual wiggle room here. Tier two priests, who were good tier two priests, did a little trysting and nookying around, but they did it well outside the parish boundaries. This was the ideal held up to me. Needless to say, I had never had the case presented to me like this in the seminary. She sealed this advice with an old Italian axiom: *chi vuol' pescare (whoever wants to fish) va a lontano (go far away) e poi pesca! (and then fish to your heart's content.)*

In other words, since I had the red blood like everyone else and, since saying Mass did not exsanguinate me, I should be honest, face the facts of life, and find the womanly companionship I obviously needed in some far-away place...*va a lontano*. I mounted further protest, telling how well trained we were for our celibate lives and how our commitment was tested in the seminary. She sighed and shook her head dismissively, uttered one more emphatic "No," and then rose and left. She gave me a parting look that seemed to say: "I've done my best. Now life will have to teach you." Thus ended the housekeeper's tale.

I shared this startling advice with my young priest friends. The Second Vatican Council was going on at that time in Rome. We decided over dinner, after a scotch or two, that it would be a capital idea to collect money and send this housekeeper over to sit with the bishops in solemn council and put some sense into their heads. We never followed through. That's the trouble with scotch-bred insights: no follow-through. Had we followed through and had La Signora housekeeper presided at the Second Vatican Council the Catholic church might not be going through many of its current travails.

Booster Shots

Because of my resistance, the housekeeper would sometimes serve us supper and then sit down and give me a follow up mini-lecture. One night it was the exciting story of a Monsignor G., a pastor in a prominent South Philly parish. From other housekeepers she knew his story well, and it was a story worth telling. (The Vatican should have learned years ago to talk to the housekeepers; then they wouldn't have had so many surprises.) It seems the red-blooded Monsignor G. began to *fare la vita,* her expression for have an affaire, with a wife in the parish. That went on unnoticed for a while but then the monsignor expanded his operation and began simultaneously to *fare la vita* with the woman's lovely young daughter. This did not go smoothly.

The wife and daughter discovered they were sharing a lover, a monsignorial lover at that, and the battle erupted. The outraged daughter was understandably miffed to learn that in her love life, she could not even trust her own mother and the mother lamented that she could even have raised such a cheater of a daughter. The husband/father heard the row. To thicken the plot which was pretty thick already, he was a Sicilian and he took poorly to this news. He was also a man of action. After loudly upbraiding the two fallen women, his attention turned to the amorous Monsignor.

One Saturday evening, the Monsignor was in the confessional box hearing other people confess their sins. The aggrieved father arrived, pulled open the confessional door, razor in hand, and slashed the face of the Monsignor, leaving him with a permanent cross-the-face scar that in Sicily was the mark of the cuckold.

Monsignor G. was a man whose lusts were only matched by his aplomb. Stitched and prominently bandaged he betook himself to Cardinal Dougherty's office the following Monday and announced: "*Io sono un martire della fede.*" "I am a martyr for the faith!" He then recounted how he was preaching the gospel to an unreceptive man who reacted violently. The cardinal took him at his word and suggested he take a two-week vacation to recover from the attack. And the resourceful Monsignor took off for the south seas.

By now I was getting into the spirit of the housekeeper's narratives and I asked if the Monsignor had taken anyone else's daughter or spouse with him on his vacation. She had no information on that.

All of these stories, confirmed by the kindly pastor of my parish with a sad nod, were intended to instruct me, the naive young priest, on how easily the celibacy bubble could burst. The stories were not limited to the Italian and Italian-American clergy. Most of the miscreant tier three priests reported on by the housekeeper were of Irish, German, or Polish Americans. In fact it was an old Irish priest who, in joking reference to priestly lapses in chastity commented cynically: "Celibacy is hard, but it sure beats no sex at all!"

Make no mistake. Many priests stayed faithful to their celibacy vow. In some cultures most did, but the system was always liable to rupture at the seams. Celibacy is just not job-related. It's not what they call in law a BFOQ, a bona fide occupational qualification. Other religions don't make it a universal mandate and life is better there and scandals fewer.

Later in my life, when I had left the priesthood and earned the title "father" in a new way, I was a visiting chair-holder for a year at the University of Notre Dame. My seven-year-old son Tommy was with me at lunch one day when we were joined by one of the Notre Dame Holy Cross Fathers. He was a delightful and warm man, and I would say, knowing him, that it was overwhelmingly likely he was fully observant of the celibacy requirement. When he left, Tommy asked. "Is he married?" "No, I replied, "They don't let priests marry." Out of the mouths of babes," as the Bible puts it, came Tommy's reply. "That's really a shame. He would be a terrific daddy!" "Yes," I replied, "and he would still be a terrific priest." My seven-year-old son, I thought proudly, has more sense than the pope. And I also thought to myself, what a shame that a healthy warm-hearted man like that should be denied the happy experience of falling in love with someone who was in love with him, a love that could be celebrated in a sexual liturgy of joyful pleasure. As one frustrated priest put it to me one time: "We're like bees being told to stay away from the flowers."

Educating Father Maguire

When I came back from Rome I thought I knew everything. If I didn't have the answer at hand, it would be in my trunk and I could get it for you. I was Mr. Smug. That didn't last long. First the Italian housekeeper began my Life 101 Reeducation Program, followed by a veritable gang bang of other instructors disrupting my tidy view of life. I fled for relief to a meeting of the Catholic Theological Society of America. There I would be safe; no housekeepers in that Society. No parishioners looking at me with an "are-you-serious" look as I explained that no sexual thoughts, words or deeds were permissible outside of marriage, even for the engaged. The rules were so clear. Why could they not understand them?

So off I went to the Catholic Theological Society meeting where I could be safe and secure, surrounded by priests like me in Roman collars…not a woman in sight back then at meetings like that. It was like being back in the seminary. On top of that there were great speakers there from Europe, where we thought all great Catholic thinking occurred. A German superstar theologian was there, a Redemptorist priest, Fr. Bernard Haring.

Haring was a leader in the updating of Catholic moral theology starting in the 1960s. Although living in Rome, he was such a diplomatic and sure-footed gentleman that he could do the work of reform right there under the Vatican's nose, and survive. His appearance was that of the grey haired gentle guru. His voice was kindly and measured, his scholarship solid. The Vatican not only trusted him but invited him to preach a retreat to the Vatican staff, pope included. Here was someone I could trust, someone who would give me ammunition to bring back to those horny young people who doubted my "abstinence only" teaching.

Some 400 Catholic theologians were in attendance. After his talk on how it would be smart to get back to the Bible—not a threatening idea I thought—he opened the floor for questions. The first question concerned the Friday abstinence rule and how much meat you could eat before it was seriously sinful…before it turned into a "mortal sin" kind of thing. Fr. Haring blew that off and said that in the United States we should rather be asking people about their racism and not their diets. I liked that. He seemed to be saying that whatever Jesus was up. to it was not a campaign against carnivores.

Of course Haring was living in Rome and, of course I had learned the Italians paid no attention to the meatless Friday rule. So I was delighted with this and felt superior to a number of old priests around me who seemed upset by this downgrading of Friday abstinence. I felt I was a cut above these fuddy-duddy old conservatives.

The next question put to Fr. Haring was a big one. It was a debate I knew about concerning sperm and how to get it for a sperm test for fertility testing. Fertility testing would seem to be close to the Catholic heart with its stress on reproduction. When a couple could not conceive fertility testing was in order. Since the problem might be the male, the doctors needed to see the condition of the sperm upon delivery. Could it, in the transit from the testicles have picked up some secretions that slowed those little swimmers down? Good question.

Big problem. How to get that sperm!

Two theories were suggested in the literature at that time. The first I would code name "the OUCH procedure." It was suggested by moral theologians that the doctor could simply insert a needle into the testicles and pull some of those sperm into a syringe. Problem solved! But no. That did not satisfy the doctors. That would merely show how the sperm was in storage, not how it was after its passage to the penis. (Pause for a moment and picture 400 theologians sitting around pondering this spermatic conundrum.)

Since the OUCH procedure did not produce what was needed, a new theory had arrived which seemed fool-proof. It involved the use of a perforated condom. Now at first blush, taking a fine condom and turning it into a leaky condom seems counterproductive and even counterintuitive. That misses the brilliance of this solution. Catholics were not allowed to use condoms since the only licit sexual intercourse required the deposit of sperm into the vagina. Blocking sperm from entering the vagina was the sin of contraception.

But notice: intercourse with a leaky condom allowed some sperm to make it into the vagina where it belonged. All that was required therefore, was for the couple to have intercourse using the leaky condom and then present the condom to the doctor for examination. Perfect. No contraceptive intercourse and lots of sperm to keep the doctor happy.

Of course, there were certain indignities involved in this maneuver. It was just a tad redolent of a stud farm operation because the couple should have intercourse in the doctor's office—not of course the front office—since they needed be in a position to give the fresh sperm to the doctor immediately, before any changes occurred in the condition of the sperm. Driving it across town would not be helpful. Mailing the leaky condom would be even worse.

Would you believe it! The theologians were bending over backwards to get the sperm to market, as it were, and medical science never seemed satisfied. Doctors pointed out that condoms are not made to be nice to sperm. There are chemical ingredients in the condom that would affect the sperm and pollute the sample.

As any fair-minded person could see, this was a terrible dilemma. We were all for fertility and therefore for fertility testing but the damned sperm was causing us big time trouble.

Solution? Ask the great Fr. Haring, the leading authority in Catholic moral theology.

The questioner put it clearly: "Fr. Haring what is the best way to get sperm for fertility testing?" We all sat in rapt silence to hear what the great theologian would say. Would he come down on the OUCH side of the debate, or the leaky condom alternative?

Fr. Haring paused just a moment, and then said: "Getting sperm for sperm testing? Massaging the penis is very effective! Are there any other questions?"

Did you ever hear stunned silence? Stunned silence is really, really quiet, as though even all breathing has been suspended. The simplicity of truth can shock like a thunder clap. I don't recall that there were any heart attacks or strokes on the spot but it had the makings of a medical emergency.

And how did young Father Maguire, that abstinence-only guy, react? I didn't begin to digest it until the flight home from St. Louis where the meeting was held, but Fr. Haring had just joined the Italian housekeeper as a major mentor. It was like clouds had lifted and simple clear common sense had flashed with sunshine brilliance. Masturbation could be OK, not morally objectionable, perfectly reasonable. Had not Thomas Aquinas said the truly reasonable is the truly good, and massaging the penis to get sperm—exactly as it would be upon delivery—just what the doctors needed—was truly reasonable.

When a change like that happens, you do not realize how changed you are. A senseless taboo has been broken and that opens the mind in ways you don't realize to the possibility that there might be other taboos out there. And sure enough, there were!

It was a somewhat less rigid Father Maguire who returned to the little parish in Southwest Philadelphia.

CHAPTER FIVE
WAKE-UP CALLS

While I was getting slightly roused from my dogmatic stupor by the famous theologian Bernard Haring, a whole parish of Philadelphians rich in the kind of life experience where I was a pauper, were lying in wait. For three or four hours on a Saturday, I would sit in a confessional box hearing their sins and learning about life. Beyond that, people would come to the rectory office to present problems that needed more than a quick fix in the confessional.

A young man came to see me one time in my parish office. A year before, he met a girl who bowled him over with her beauty and gentle charm. As soon as they went out on their first date, a large problem surfaced. She had been given terrible, neuroticizing lessons about her body and her sexuality. The slightest touch of a hand, the slightest hint of intimacy, panicked her. Kissing or embracing was out of the question. Let's face it. A male in the heat of first love could be turned off by this. This marvel of a young man was not. Instead he eased her embarrassment, telling her that there were lots of fun things they could do together, skating, skiing, going to shows, and walking in the park. And so for months they were together on a no-touch, no hanky-panky regimen. During this time they saw a lot of one another and grew more deeply in love. And yet an icy wall of fear, her fear of her sexuality stood between them.

As love grew, trust grew, and a beautiful thaw commenced as peacefully as dawn banishes the night. It happened spontaneously. At an emotional moment in a movie, he reached for her hand without thinking and she gripped it tightly. No panic, no pulling way. They left the theater holding hands as joyfully as hands were ever held. The healing had begun in a context of patient and exquisite love.

The healing continued at an unrushed pace. When the young man came to see me, they were engaged with a marriage scheduled six months later. Their intimacy had proceeded to petting and his fiancée had begun to experience orgasm.

So why was this young man coming to see me when everything was going so swimmingly? Because in the rigid theology of the day, what they were doing was mortal sin and an offense against God. That was my view too. His argument was that if they suddenly stopped this intimacy the old ghosts would return and the sweet process of healing and sexual joy would be jolted. He wanted to continue being intimate in this way, even before the wedding.

No way, said I. I then unwrapped all my arguments, telling him that there is a marital package of sexual privileges and they were breaking into that package. The Vatican was speaking through me. He and his fiancée, I said, were assuming rights that they did not have. After an hour of my best efforts, he was unconvinced and kept returning to the beauty of their relationship in all of its expressions.

A Distant Light Flashing in the Night

We were both exhausted at this point, and my exhaustion was complicated by a growing uneasiness with the very arguments I was mouthing. They must be right. I had passed exams on them and did well and yet, in the face of this man and his stirring story of tender love, my well learned arguments seemed anemic. It was then that I was jolted awake by memory. There is a tradition I had studied in theology classes, but never applied; it is called Probabilism. In a nutshell this old Catholic gem said that on debated moral issues you could dissent from "official teaching" if you could find five or six theologians known for their "prudence and learning," who held a more liberal view on that issue. This was so even if all the other ten thousand theologians held the more rigorous view, including all the bishops and popes. You were free to go with the five or six well established liberal thinkers. That was no help to this young man since neither I nor any other Catholic theologian had published a liberal view on premarital sex at that time. But there was another part to Probabilism, the do-it-yourself part, which is stunningly liberal, not something you would expect in such an authoritarian tradition. This part of Probabilism said, that if you yourself had good reasons to dissent, reasons that were "compelling, non-frivolous, of the sort that would appeal to a reasonable and good person, not self-serving," then you had what they called an "intrinsically probable opinion," and your conscience was free, and no church authority and no Father Maguire could take your moral freedom away.

As the light flashed in my brain I realized that I was sitting there looking at an "intrinsically probable opinion." His reasons were not just compelling; they were knocking me off my chair. I then gave my first lesson on Probabilism to a young man whose sweet love had brought healing to the woman he loved. He was an eager student because he already instinctively knew the wisdom I had learned but never understood or applied until that moment. I told him to bring in his fiancée and I would explain all this to her too.

As we parted and I went upstairs to my room, I knew I had done something good and I was also scared to death. My first instinct was to pour a glass of scotch and sit down to think about it. I was out on a limb. I could not think of any one of my colleagues who would agree with me, and yet I was simply applying a piece of Roman Catholic teaching on the sacredness of conscience. I was nervous, but deep down I knew I had done the right thing. A peaceful night's sleep followed as confirmation.

Dominoes Falling

Many a lecture I have given on Probabilism ever since. Once I was lecturing at Trinity College Dublin in the 1980s to an audience of some 500 Irish Catholics. I decided to do Probabilism and apply it to issues like contraception, abortion, remarriage after divorce, gay marriage—all hot spots in Catholic pelvic theology. I could see all those Irish faces looking and listening intently, but I was anxiously wondering whether I was about to be run out of the hall. The first question after my talk put me at ease. With a heavy Irish accent, showing a bit of a Galway lilt, a woman of mature years asked: "Why in God's holy name were we not told that!!??" Good question. Respect for conscience was right there in the heart of the Catholic system, but its teaching had been suppressed. So successfully suppressed that even when I had learned it, and passed exams on it, I never thought of applying it, until a gentle man with common sense and a great heart brought me to my senses.

In both church and in state, the principles that favor control are stressed over those that favor freedom and since most people don't really want to be free, the suppression works very well. Nothing is more hurtful to a church or a nation than too little dissent and too little heresy.

Virgin to Non-Virgins

Gall could hardly be made of sterner stuff. Fresh and new in the parish,

I decided that I should give a two-day retreat to the married people in the parish. There I was, a horny 28-year-old virgin, going to instruct these people on their marriages and their sexual lives. Fr. Amateis thought it a noble idea and he even attended my talks. Unfortunately he was an old man and "full of sleep," as the poet Yeats put it, and he slept through most of my very earnest talks, which was unhelpful—but for him, probably, a mercy. It was the people who were awake who suffered.

The worst sin of this arrogant effort of mine happened when I did a talk on birth control, "the cancer of marriage" I called it. In a brutal example of emotional blackmail, I pulled out something that was circulating in Catholic circles back in the 1950s and 1960s. It was a short piece called: "Letter from an Unborn Son." Its target was birth control and, of course, abortion. It was vicious.

"I know, Mom and Dad, that you didn't have me because you wanted that new car and that new refrigerator. But that car and that refrigerator will never run up and put their little arms around you as I would have if only you had chosen me."

When I read it, I remember one woman crying audibly. How embarrassing it must have been for her. I knew that she had four children and she and her husband had very little income from his humble job. I'm sure that afterwards when I went to my room and poured a little scotch for myself that I would have thought that this is what happens when you preach the gospel and touch hearts. Of course, the gospels did not give one damn about birth control or abortion, but that hadn't dawned on me yet.

The dawning did occur, and soon, as real people living real lives broke through my learned ignorance. I was becoming uneasy about some of these teachings but it seemed impossible that my brilliant teachers could be wrong. Uneasiness is important, and is often the first flickering of insight.

One couple in particular put me over the top. They were a young couple. She was pregnant and they had a toddler, and the husband was in graduate school. They were clearly maxed out on kids at this moment. Because of that they left the Catholic Church and joined a Presbyterian Church so that they could find support for their contraception.

However, they missed the Catholic liturgies and their friends in the parish, and so they came to me to plead their contraceptive case. They argued that the church was wrong on contraception. They had known me and we were friendly with one another, and so they thought they would give it a try. The woman did most of the talking. She was eloquent and calm and very insistent. Of course, I knew they were wrong but I would give them a hearing. I'm nice that way.

She had a two-pronged argument. How could I call good, that which was harmful, and secondly, how could I call good, that which was unreasonable.

My blood pressure started to elevate. She didn't know it, but she was quoting Thomas Aquinas, one of my favorite authors. Most people think of Thomas as the last word in conservatism, but that only confirms once again that conservatives are often the worshipers of dead liberals. A lot in Thomas is hideously out of date and dead wrong, but he was a bold thinker in his day. Indeed, he was the most heavily censured theologian of his time. His inaugural lecture at the University of Paris was boycotted and his books were banned. He dared to read pagan authors like Aristotle, a no-no in his time. I always found a lot in Thomas that thrilled my mind. I just had not applied most of his good stuff to reality.

Now here was this woman, a high school graduate, saying things to me out of her own mind that I could have given back to her in Latin from the pages of Thomas' *Summa Theologiae*.

Our long session ended without my conceding anything, but my timbers had been rattled. I needed time. I kept going over the arguments I had learned. The prime purpose of sex is procreation; all other purposes are secondary and thus sex can never be used non-procreatively. To do so violates the natural law. Yet, the words of this woman continued vibrating and their Thomistic good sense haunted me.

I find that most intellectual breakthroughs come after a good sleep. I had a good sleep and was driving on the Schuylkill Expressway at around 65 miles an hour when the lightning struck. I went through the old arguments against birth control for the umpteenth time, but this time they fell apart. Reproduction is not the primary purpose of sex. Only a couple of times in a lifetime should sex have anything to do with reproduction. It has so many other joyful purposes and it is those that are primary. And very often reproduction is the worst possible outcome of sex, as when people are not ready for the 25 plus years of commitment that pregnancy commands. "We were wrong," I shouted aloud in my car, and it is a wonder I didn't plunge into the river because I was shaken to the quick.

I called the couple in and told them how they and Thomas Aquinas brought me to this shift. I told them I could not say this publicly or I would be drummed out of the priesthood in the morning, but I welcomed them and their contraceptive plans back into the church. We embraced, and I cried and so did they. And little did I know the tectonic plates that had just shifted a little further.

My next thought: the woman I had reduced to tears when I assaulted her conscience during my retreat two years before. I was due to leave the parish shortly and I had this healing business to attend to first. I asked her to come in and see me. She had very little schooling and I knew I could not go into Thomas Aquinas and the arguments in moral theology that I had worked through. Instead, paternalistic as it was, I decided to use good old

Catholic language that she would understand, no argumentation needed. I talked "dispensation."

I began our conversation asking if she remembered the retreat I had given two years before. She said she did and she said it was wonderful. I marveled that she could say that, given what I had done to her. I got swiftly to the point. "I remember," I said, "that when I spoke of contraception, you got upset." "Yes, Father," she said and started to get upset again, saying "we're poor and we spend all we have on our four children." "Wait," I said. "I have good news for you. I can give you a dispensation to practice birth control for the rest of your marriage if you wish to." Her mouth dropped open and she began to smile. I said that this is a private dispensation and must be kept confidential, so she should not tell anyone else about it.

Her next question is a stunner and an example of the power clergy can have over other peoples' minds. She asked in all earnestness: "Can I tell my husband?"

I had to laugh and I said of course you can. I then said I wanted them to both come to me for confession and then to come to my Mass to receive communion. I wanted to drape this "dispensation" of mine with all the power of the church's symbols and liturgy so that they would feel the full refreshment of a conscience at peace.

That said, we both sat there in the office silent for a moment as though exhausted by what had just transpired. I broke the silence clumsily saying "So what will you do now?"

She threw her head back as though she were speaking to the ceiling and the words erupted: "I'm going to start enjoying sex again!" She blushed immediately and winced, waving a hand in the air, as though looking for an eraser she could use to blot her words out of the ether.

In truth, I don't think she did keep this good news quiet. Good news is hard to embargo. I had more than a few more quiet requests for "dispensa-tions" in that parish before I made my getaway, and I granted them all with a somewhat nervous magnanimity. Soon, when posted in a university, my dissent would go public and that would lead to ructions galore!

IF THERE IS NO ROOM FOR
CHARLIE IN THE CATHOLIC
UNIVERSITY OF AMERICA
THERE IS NO ROOM FO
THE CATHOLIC UNIVERSIT
IN
AMERICA

CHAPTER SIX
THE GREAT ESCAPE

T hings were getting too hot for me in the Archdiocese of Philadelphia. I had already gone rogue, handing out dispensation to use condoms and sanctioning sex before marriage. I was behaving as if I thought I was the pope or something. It was time to move, so I got an appointment to teach at St. Mary's Seminary and University in Baltimore. I was now doing graduate level teaching, something I always wanted. In those days the seminaries were still packed to the gills with wonderful idealistic young men. Years later, I still hear from many of them, about half of them still priests, the other half out of the priesthood and married.

My seminary professor tour was not destined to last long. The rector there, a conservative rigid man, began to sniff early on that I had some unwelcome views. Nevertheless, while I was still surviving there, I had great experiences. One of them involved

A Cardinal, A Priest, and a Dead Wife

Cardinal Laurence Sheehan came to dinner one night at the seminary. It was at that time that the pope was preparing his encyclical on contraception and speculation was rife on what he would say. At dinner, the cardinal expressed himself freely…and enigmatically. He said he hoped the pope would end the ban on contraceptives. However, he quickly added that if he did not he would fully accept whatever the pope said. I guess that is what it takes to be a cardinal. He wanted the teaching to change, showing that he thought it was wrong and should be changed, but if the pope refused to do so, he would go along with it and still preach the wrong stuff.

Shortly thereafter I had dinner with a priest in Baltimore. He was an honest and sincere man but very conservative. I mentioned over dinner the cardinal's expressed wish that the pope would change the teaching on birth control. The priest panicked and became terribly upset. "They can't change that teaching," he said; " if they do I am a murderer."

That was a rather stunning claim. I awaited his explanation. Two years before a couple came to him with this problem. They were in their 20s and had just had a baby. However, the pregnancy was difficult in the extreme, requiring frequent hospitalization. The doctor said he could not continue to attend her if she became pregnant again since he did not think she could survive another pregnancy in her condition. The priest told them they had two options: they could practice the rhythm method, confining intercourse to supposedly non-fertile times of the month, or they could just decide on a "Josephite marriage" where they would have no sex at all.

(Calling sexless marriage Josephite underestimates the Joseph to whom Luke's gospel refers as Jesus' parent. In addition Mark's gospel mentions the four brothers of Jesus and his sisters. So, according to the gospels, Mary and Joseph did not have one of those "Josephite marriages" and as a couple of well adjusted Jews would probably have thought the idea pretty damned foolish.)

Anyhow, the young couple decided on the rhythm method. The wife became pregnant and she died. Obviously the right solution was sterilization of either or, for security, of both partners, but contraceptive sterilization was also banned by the old teaching.

If the teaching the priest gave her caused that death, and if that teaching were wrong, the priest felt like a murderer who had been betrayed by the teaching church. He betook himself forthwith to the cardinal to make his case. I later got a letter from the cardinal professing his complete belief in whatever the pope should decide in the coming encyclical. For the cardinal, if the pope said up is down, he would go along with that formulation. Talk about malleability!

Next Stop

After two years it became clear to me that I had no lasting home in a seminary. I was offered a position at The Catholic University of America, a university where academic freedom was supposed to be sacred. I jumped at the opportunity and thus began five of the most exciting years of my life. To teach at Catholic University in those days was a battlefield. Those of us teaching theology should have received combat pay. Most university professors pass their entire lives without having to face a formal academic dismissal trial.

I faced two of them in five years.

Catholic University in Washington is a special kind of place. All the cardinals in the United States are on its board of trustees and the Archbishop of D.C. is the Chancellor. That creates a "heavy, heavy what hangs over" atmosphere. At the same time there was electricity in the air. Pope John XXIII had convened the Second Vatican Council to "let a little fresh air" through the "windows of the church." The *Zeitgeist* was right for it.

Hunger for fresh air was growing everywhere in the 1960s from the Communist empire through the politics of the West. The atmosphere at Catholic University was electric, like the mood of a just awakened Rip Van Winkle. People would come out of one theology class asking what had happened in other classes. Walls were crumbling and light was shining where it had never shone before.

Pope Paul VI promised an encyclical on contraception. There was hope for a change. We wise theologians, drunk on the times, were sure the encyclical would open the door to contraception and relieve the needlessly tortured consciences of Catholics. We had reason to hope, since the word was out that the committee the pope had convened to advise him on the issue had voted overwhelmingly to say the church was wrong to ban contraception.

Sorry About That

The encyclical was to be released on an August night in 1968. I was in Washington and my close colleague Charles Curran was hiding out upstate in New York working on a book and studying German. In spite of our hopes, we knew the pope could blow it. Talking by phone, we prepared a plan in case the encyclical disappointed us. If it does we agreed, "we'll blow the lid off!"

The world press was lying in wait, ready to pounce on every word of this document to see if the turnaround had happened. Curran and I agreed to listen to the morning news starting as 6:00 a.m. and if by 8:00 a.m. the news was bad, we would spring into action. If worse came to worst—and it did—Curran would call me and we would meet in Washington, get the full document in its original Latin and if it is as bad as it sounds from press reports, start organizing a theological revolt.

In fact, the press had it right. The pope was shutting the door, ignoring his own committee majority, and reasserting the taboo. At 8:05 my phone rang and I assumed it was Charlie Curran. I picked up the phone and sang into it the opening verses of an old Catholic hymn: "Long live the Pope his praises sing, again and yet again." (It's not a hymn you hear much anymore.) After my outburst there was silence for a moment on the other end of the line and then a voice said: "Father, this is Russ Chandler of the *Los Angeles Times*." I laughed and said, "Well you've got my statement. What more do you need?" He laughed and I then gave him a lot more, telling him the pope was dead wrong and we were not going to receive this in silence.

Back in Caldwell Hall at Catholic University, after scouring the document in Latin and in English and after consulting with colleagues, Charlie Curran and I sat at his decrepit old typewriter (the Andy Rooney kind) and banged out a statement of dissent telling Catholics that they were free to disagree with the prohibition of contraception in this papal document. We then got on the phone to get other theologians to sign it. Within days we had over 600 teachers of theology risking their careers, telling Catholic couples that they were free to make up their own minds on family planning. It was international news and also a moment without precedent in American Catholic life. The pope's response was gentle. He commented that he saw that his encyclical had engendered "a lively debate."

The Trials

Catholic University, hell bent on "orthodoxy," instituted an academic trial of its 21 dissenting priest professors. The prestigious law firm of Cravath, Swaine, and Moore, under the leadership of attorney John Hunt came down to defend "the twenty-one subject professors" on a *pro bono* basis. We survived and indeed triumphed before a jury of academic peers.

A few years later, I decided to leave the priesthood and marry. That led to another academic trial. This time I did not survive. Committing matrimony was more than Catholic University could endure. Even though my action was described by one cardinal as a "lamentable defection," Marquette

University, under the leadership of two Jesuits, John Raynor and Quentin Quesnell, hired me and I have been there ever since, disquieting some and pleasing others. However, there was still more excitement at Catholic University before I was ousted.

On Strike

In 1967, something happened at Catholic University that has not happened in any other modern university known to me. We went on strike and shut the place down.

My friend Charles Curran in the 1960s was one of the first priest theologians to publish liberal views on sexual and reproductive issues. His scholarship was deep-rooted, which made him terribly threatening to the hierarchy. He came up for tenure and promotion to associate professor in 1967. The Board of Trustees, peopled with many cardinals and bishops decided to sack Charlie. Heretofore, that was the way they dealt with professors who came up with something original. But this was in the bubbling sixties and it was spring and the sap was running. Bowing to authorities was not in vogue. "We're all fed up. Ain't goin' to take it any more" was a civil rights mantra on the streets: "resist authority" was in the air and in the water. The moment was ripe for revolution. And revolution happened at the Catholic University of America, the national university of the Catholic Church with special affiliation to the Vatican.

First, the theology department voted to go on strike, issuing this statement: "We cannot and will not function unless and until Father Curran is reinstated. We invite our colleagues in other schools of the university to join with us in our protest." An informational meeting was held at which some of us spoke. The final words in my little speech were: "If there is no room for Charlie in the Catholic University of America, there is no room for the Catholic University in America." As the strike began, two nuns in full religious garb—one of them the sister of an archbishop—put this message on a huge poster and carried in the marches of the next few days. The picture appeared in the *New York Times*. (cf. page 69)

All of us told our classes that we were going to call for a strike. The students asked sharp questions. Why were they after Curran? One student asked me: "Does this guy have a chick on the side or something?" I assured him there were no skeletons in this closet. The full faculty met in the McMahon auditorium with more than 3,000 students outside awaiting their decision on the strike. The vote was 400 to 18 to shut down the university. A roar went up from the students outside when the word reached them.

There is a long sign with big letters outside the university entrance, The Catholic University of America. The students posted a white strip across it saying CLOSED. That and the marching strikers were on TV every day.

The students were magnificent. This was the sixties. Long hair was *de rigeur.* Knowing that they were going to be on TV every day many of the male students decided to get haircuts to make their protest more palatable to conservatives who stigmatized long hair on men. Professors long since retired, now on walkers, returned to join the daily marches. Television cameras followed our every move.

In five days the trustees folded. Two cardinals, Sheehan in Baltimore and Cushing in Boston publicly criticized the action against Curran. A friend told me that Cardinal Cody of Chicago in his own gruff style said: "Get those Goddamned kids off television and back in the classroom." (He had voted to fire Curran.) Curran was rehired, promoted and tenured. and a booming celebration followed.

The Vatican waited. The centuries breed patience. Then in 1986 Joseph Cardinal Ratzinger, now Pope Benedict XVI, speaking from the office once known as the Office of the Inquisition, declared with the approval of Pope

John Paul II, that Curran was no longer "eligible or suitable" to teach Catholic theology. Catholic University buckled and Curran, a full professor with tenure and a stellar reputation as a scholar, was fired. There was no strike this time. It was no longer the sixties. The Catholic University swallowed its integrity, dumped Curran, violated his legal rights, and put a cloud over all the academic degrees it would subsequently award. A court case followed and Curran lost, showing the lenience the courts in theocratic America will allow for religious violations of contracts and rights. (Only in our day is that changing in trials of church officials in clergy sex abuse cases. No bishops have yet gone to jail, and they should. It was they who managed the coverup of clergy sexual abuse that victimized thousands of children. So far the hierarchy have not behaved as well as Penn State University in their response to a single abuser, unlike the thousands of victims the church failed to protect.)

Curran moved to a distinguished professorship at Southern Methodist University. The Methodists down there are not dumb.

Heart Smarts

When we were not on strike or on trial, we did a lot of teaching at Catholic University. It was exciting. Most students were open to new liberal ideas, but some were terrified, fearing the operation was on the skids. We had to dodge administrators and deal with irate conservatives within and without the university

My very first class at Catholic University had 75 students in it. Most were priests, nuns, and seminarians, with a sprinkling of laity. Part of the course was on marriage. My studies had convinced me that the old church teaching on divorce was wrong. "Til death do us part" come hell or high water did not meet the facts of life. I began by showing how the anti-divorce teaching of Jesus related to a time when divorce was mainly an issue of male exploitation of women and exploitation was the central target of Jesus and the prophets of Israel. I explained why Jesus took a hard line on divorce. In his day a divorced woman was a pariah, destined for poverty and social stigma. His position was not one binding for all time and different circumstances.

The Bible does not say that a person can't try again after a failed marriage. I was moving the class slowly showing how literal readings of the Bible were deceptive. It was clear from the start where I was going and I could feel a growing unease in the class. My conclusion was not going to be welcomed.

There was a happy ending in this class and it had nothing to do with my scholarship.

A friend contacted me about her cousin Jack and his wife Sally. Here is their story and how it turned a class of Catholic clergy and religious upside down.

Jack was always thought of in the family as a dear but pretty self-centered guy, and a bit of a cheapskate. Then the seismic shifts of love shook his earth. When the family went out for pizza on their weekly bowling night, Jack would insist they sit where a woman named Sally was the waitress. Jack also insisted on one and all leaving huge tips for Sally. Obviously Jack was gaga over Sally and it was clear that Sally was as smitten as he.

Sally had been married to a violent man. They had two children and the kids also were abused by their father. Sally, a Catholic, stayed on the principle that she took him before God for better or worse; she was getting worse, but could not break the vow of fidelity. When a third child was born showing some of the effects of the beatings Sally suffered during the pregnancy, Sally finally bolted. She took the job as a waitress, and got as much help as she could protecting herself and her kids from the aggressive father. During this time she met Jack and they fell in love. Problem: according to the then-official Catholic teaching, she was not marriageable until her former husband died.

Deeply in love as they were, they could see no permanent future for their relationship. Therefore, she and Jack repeatedly and tearfully tried to break up. The breakup would last a couple of weeks and then one would call the other, just to see how the other was doing. The magnetism of passionate love would not brook separation and quickly they would reunite.

Finally they stopped struggling and got married by a Justice of the Peace. This was not easy for 1960s Catholics. They were now "living in sin." Sin or not, life got better. Jack was a powerfully built man and when the ex-husband made an effort to enter their home, he ended up sitting in the middle of the street where he could contemplate the foreseeable effects of any other attempted visits. Better yet, Jack got a job offer in Phoenix, and now the ex-husband was history. Through all of this Jack became a loving daddy of the three children of another man. One of the children who had been in therapy due to the violence of the old home situation, was now well. This was a healing household, and the previously immature Jack was perhaps the most healed of all. Still, it was not a "happily ever after" story because of the religious stigma they endured.

Then a crisis occurred. Sally got pregnant and a tumor was detected that required surgery. She feared the worst and wanted to be spiritually at peace before going to the hospital. She went to a priest in confession, and it was a rigid and strict priest she found. He told her she would have to renounce Jack, the love of her life, and the loving care-giver to her children. Jack would have to go if Sally was to return to the sacraments of the church. They were desperate. That's when Jack's cousin called me.

Happy Ending

Now back to my Catholic University class and my efforts to teach about remarriage after divorce. I came in and told the class the story of Jack and Sally with all of its pain and poignancy. I told them that the solution was in what I had been teaching them. Permanent marriage is the ideal but the ideal does not always happen. Clearly it was happening in this second marriage of Sally's. I told them what I thought should be done, not mentioning that I myself intended to do it. I said a priest should go out there and tell Jack and Sally that he could bless their marriage. Although this was forbidden at the time, he should celebrate Mass in their home and conduct a full Catholic wedding ceremony, giving them the sacraments they had been long denied. He should then perform a Catholic wedding service for them, and allow Sally to face her surgery in peace.

There was a deadly stillness as I spoke. I could not judge how this departure from normal Catholic practice was being received. Then the bell rang, ending the class. Up to the desk marched an angry looking nun in full robes. I expected damnation. Instead, she said: "Don't stand there talking about it. Get a priest out there immediately and help these people!" I told her we were working on that. Right behind her was a quiet little priest who had never opened his mouth throughout the course. He moved close to me and said, in a hushed voice: "I am a priest of the Phoenix diocese and I am going there tomorrow after your test and will be happy to do everything you said." Just as quietly, I leaned over and said to him: "Father, skip the test: you just got an A!" He had just demonstrated that he understood everything I had taught.

The next day was the last class preceding the afternoon test. All 75 students were there. I told them that a priest in this class was going to fly there the next day to do the deed. I would not, of course, identify him. The class erupted into a standing ovation clapping for their unidentified classmate. And the shy little priest with a face of red stood with them clapping clumsily for himself.

I then gave the class my conclusion: permanent marriage is the ideal but the ideal is not to be used as a club to batter people who manage to realize that ideal in a second or third marriage. Notes were taken and not an objection was raised. And who was the teacher? The real life needs of Jack and Sally got into the hearts of my listeners and 75 Catholics came of age. My lectures could not have done it. I needed Jack and Sally.

And what of Sally's tumor? It was benign, surgery was successful, and the baby was born well. But that was not the end of it. Twenty years later Jack and Sally moved to a new parish, and some sharp priest noted that there was no official record of their church wedding. Jack's family called me. I was now a professor at the Jesuit Marquette University.

Here's how I handled it. Any system of law that has survived a long time has wiggle room in it, including Catholic canon law. Solutions are sometimes allowed in extraordinary circumstances. Accommodations can be reached *in foro interno*, privately, when the normal procedures are impossible.

I got out my university stationery, invoked the relevant canon law, and assured the priest that I had been the theological counselor for their wedding which was fully valid and sacramental and should be so recorded. The priest was satisfied. He had a piece of paper saying that everything was kosher. And with that, the happily ever after continued for Jack and Sally. And I as a teacher learned again the role of feeling and compassion in getting to the truth.

Hiding Behind Aquinas

Saint Thomas Aquinas is a Catholic super-hero. Canon law even said that on any disputed issue, if you had Aquinas on your side, you were fine. Much in Aquinas is awful, and typical of his thirteenth century world. But he was a rebel and a pusher of new ideas and I studied him well and quoted him often. Thomas was one of the most heavily censured intellectuals of his day. His inaugural lecture at the University of Paris was boycotted, his books were banned, and bishops blasted him. He broke ranks with fellow Christians who would not read pagan authors like Aristotle. Later, better sense prevailed and Thomas was canonized a saint and given top billing in the Catholic cast of theological stars. With Catholics at the time of my talk, he was bigger than Bible...and I fled into his protective arms often.

There were several Irish priests in my class who loved to do spoofs of the professors at departmental parties. One of the verses they sang to me went like this:

> *Apparently Aquinas*
> *is not so bad at all*
> *Because Dan always quotes him*
> *when his back's against the wall!*

Once I was asked to speak at a convention of Washington D.C. Catholic religious educators and my back was really against the wall. The invitation had escaped the notice of Cardinal O'Boyle but it was too late to change the program by cancelling the main speaker. My subject was "What's New in Moral Theology?" This was in the 1960s and a lot was new and shocking on issues like birth control, abortion, remarriage after divorce, same-sex marriage and the right to conscientious objection to an ongoing war. Since it was too late to sack me, the cardinal instead sent a monsignor from his office to open the event with a prayer and to sit in the first row right in front of my rostrum as a kind of visible on-site defender of the faith.

With the Grand Inquisitor in front of me, I decided to go ahead anyhow and open the door on all those controversial issues, but I made one strategic switch. I dropped all references to every source except Saint Thomas Aquinas.

In this talk, I constantly quoted Thomas, often in Latin as well as in English. This was not to show off. This was to have the talk dripping with Thomistic authority in all of its primeval Latinity. The monsignor seemed a tad bewildered but friendly afterwards when he shook my hand. Later, a priest friend of mine in the cardinal's office told me that the monsignor reported back to the surprised cardinal: "The man is actually orthodox." My neck, for the moment, was spared. "Apparently Aquinas is not so bad at all."

CHAPTER SEVEN
GETTING CHILDED

The first chill winds of autumn had arrived but the leaves had not yet begun to turn. Our son Tom was around three and a very vocal presence. We called him "the speaker of the house." From things he had said, I realized that he had no recollection of the autumnal miracle of colors. He had been otherwise engaged and took no note of the marvels of Fall.

I came upon him one day in the den. He was standing at his usual post with his thumb in his mouth (preparing an orthodontic bill for me), with his cloth dog "Patches" in his arms. I went over and asked him: "Tommy, what color are those leaves on the trees out back?" Out came the thumb and he replied: "Green." "Tommy," I continued, "do you know what is going to happen soon, in a few weeks?" The thumb came out again and he looked up waiting to hear. I said: "All of those leaves are going to change colors, some will be red, some orange, or brown, or yellow. Then all of them will fall off the tree." He looked at me intently and I wondered if he thought the old man had finally lost it. Back went the thumb. No comment.

The next day I was passing the den when I heard Tommy at his window post talking to Patches. This is a precious parental moment and I crept close to the den door to eavesdrop. With a voice filled with awe and reverence, I heard Tommy's address to Patches. "Patches, all leaves green. All leaves turn red, orange, yellow, brown. All fall down!" The colors were memorized. I suddenly realized how total was his belief in me and my word. If I had said: "Tommy, soon all those trees out there will pull up from the ground, turn upside down and hang there in the air for the winter," Tommy would have relayed that gospel with full faith and verbatim to Patches. I was his pope, his infallible guru, his Bible, his Qur'an, his contact with reality. If I were wrong the world is chaos and so he clung with pious fervor to my version of reality.

Believe or Else

It has been said that all kids need to be parented, and all parents (indeed all adults) need to be childed. Kids are teachers as well as the taught. I had two little boys on my mentoring team. Tommy had just taught me a lesson on why people are so credulous, why we believe the hype—from advertisers, politicians, clergy, *et al.* We got our start in life as believers, naive, dependent, credulous believers. We arrive in life with only two sources of knowledge. One source—and a really impressive one—is sense experience. That's how we know that ice is cold and ovens are hot and floors are hard. Sense experience is so immediate, so direct in its lessons that one would think that nothing in the world could trump it. Wrong. There is another source of truth: those towering people on whom we are utterly and totally dependent for everything. When our billions of cells cry out in hunger, those giants are all we have going for us. When we're cold, they warm us; when we hurt they hold us.

When they talk, we listen.

I saw this clearly when I watched two little boys being born. Getting born is one big pain. Clearly the birth canal was not fashioned with us in mind. From a cozy setting with womb services always available, we get evicted into a world of squashing and hurt with bright lights and cold metal with our erstwhile host crying in pain. What a revolting development!

If you could put words on those two little faces emerging at birth, it would be *"what the hell is going on!?"* That's the beginning of philosophy because that's all the philosophers and theologians have ever been asking. We get born asking it. We are, as the Greeks say, *philosophoi*, lovers and needers of wisdom and knowledge right from birth. We need to know.

For a while we have no choice but to be un-skeptical believers. Growing up is moving beyond that and a lot of people don't bother. Our reliance on authorities can be so great that in bizarre cases we may end up feeding poisoned Kool Aid to ourselves and our children in Jonestown on orders from our guru. Educated journalists and their readers will accept government propaganda as though it descended numinously wrapped from Olympus, although all they are doing is recycling garbage. Soldiers will march to their death relying blindly on their leaders' definition of the mission. Weep not for cultists but weep for ourselves since there is a bit of the cultist in us all.

When I was a student in Rome in the 1950s, I came upon a French theologian Henri De Lubac. His stuff was not at all that wild, but he was prying open some little windows. I smelled excitement there, faint hints of new horizons. I started to read him hungrily. Then I learned that he had been condemned in Pope Pius XII's encyclical, *Humani Generis*. Bye, bye De Lubac! I tossed the book. I was busy and could not waste time reading what was wrong. My interpretation of Catholicism at that time was cultist. I had started to taste liberating truth, but I bowed without question to the authority of the leader. If the leader said the leaves were going to turn various colors, then change they would.

Thinking for one's self is a second birth and most people would rather not do that again. Easier to get someone to do it for you. The preacher James Dobson has been pope to millions. He'll think for you and millions line up for his services on three thousand radio stations. So many people wrote in for his books and pamphlets that the government had to give him his own zip code. This Pope thing...the Ayatollah thing, it's pan-human.

Danny and the Birds

My son Danny was retarded, profoundly so, ravaged by Hunter's Syndrome which would end his life at age ten. And yet, he too was my teacher. I remember the day I took Danny to the beautiful lagoon near our home. We got out of the car. Danny suddenly saw the colorful mallard ducks and the birds of many kinds and colors. He was appropriately stunned. He stopped, grabbed my leg and shouted in appreciative amazement "Daddy, look, Daddy look!!" In the eulogy when Danny died, I cited this as Danny's valedictory to a world more retarded than he. Look, please look! We don't look at what we have and we don't see what we are wrecking. Danny with all his mental brokenness was more capable of appropriate ecstasy.

Danny was diagnosed at twenty-two months. Prior to that his life was joy without shadow. Then an observant doctor tolled the knell, predicting his death "early in the second decade" of his life and so it was to be. This lively little toddler was terminally ill, with no cure in sight. The immediate gift Danny gave all of us who were pained on a daily basis by his prospective death was a new respect for the present tense. In most cultures, people live fleetingly, reaching for the next before the now is done. Danny's *now* focused all our minds. There was no indefinite future to distract from his still delightful present. We got better at *looking*, to develop what the Buddhists call attentiveness, to relish each moment with him since his temporaryness was now a diagnosed fact. A hard lesson Danny taught, but a good one. There is nothing that focuses your mind like the knowledge that your child will soon die.

The Buddhist Thich Nhat Hanh noted that when we drink tea we gulp it down while we are distracted by conversation or reading, multi-tasking instead of enjoying the tea. By so doing, says Thich Nhat Hanh we do violence to the tea, to the moment, and to ourselves. As the Taoists remind us, even sex can be badly done in an *ASAP* rush. We fast-food it, rather than awaiting as Taoist wisdom counsels, for the "heavenly moment" when "high sex" can be celebrated and given its unrushed banquet due.

Pathos and Laughter

Laughter is an analgesic. Small wonder the pained do a lot of it.

With the balm of humor, the sour can become sweet and wounds can heal. A woman once told me of a turning point in her marriage. Things were not going well. The kids had been sick. The car was failing. The roof had a small leak. Debts were piling up. They both woke around 5:00 am, two hours before they needed to get up. Each knew the other was awake but they lay there in silence. The prospective gloom of another day hung over the bed. After some minutes of this the wife on a sudden happy impulse, threw her arm up in the air and then plopped it on her husband's chest blurting out: "Oh shit, honey, we're in this mess together!" Both of them roared with laughter as they embraced—and then I don't know what they went on to do and that's certainly none of our business. She referred to that early morning laugh as "the turning point in our marriage."

Agony and Ecstasy

Kids can save you from your all-too-serious self. My sister Kate who had a big Catholic family of seven kids says that kids in their first three years have paid you back in laughs for all the trouble they might cause you later. (This is the same Kate who says grandchildren are the reward you get for not having killed your children…witnessing to the fact that kids are not all laughs!)

It may surprise and sadden the reader to learn that sometimes my superior wisdom is rejected at meetings at my university. After one such atrocity, I was stormy mad as I drove home. I carried my rage into the house and started venting. As though an alarm had sounded, the two little ones on hearing my rant rushed into the kitchen pulling me away and shouting "Stop talking, Daddy...play horsey." I wanted to keep on with my righteous protesting but the kids forbade it. Soon I was on my knees in the hall with two riders trying to mount me simultaneously. The evening turned to laughter. When the boys were bathed and lying contentedly in their beds recharging their batteries, I had to stop and ask myself what I had been so upset about. The evening had been rescued and sweetened by the instinctive reaction of two little boys, one of them with a blighted mind but exquisite affections, and both with brilliant inborn instincts for peace over pain, for fun over outrage.

Danny died when Tommy was seven and the gentleness Tom has today was nourished back then. It is no easy thing to grow up with a dying brother. Tommy had to be taught to forgive Danny when Danny would break his toys or knock over his blocks.

One day I was watching the two of them in the back yard and Tommy was riding his little fire engine. He bumped into Danny and knocked him down. I rushed out to comfort the crying little victim. I scolded Tommy on how bad it was to hurt Danny and I added that as a result he would not get the expected treat.

Tommy sat there, full of grief over the lost treat...and maybe with a bit of guilt. My final words to Tommy were these: "Tommy you have to realize that Danny is a poor little guy." Tommy, thumb in mouth, thought about that for a minute and then uttered this devastating and overwhelming defense; "I a poor lil' guy too!" I, the judge, was felled by the force of that summation. (Tommy got the treat.)

A friend, Jan Sandison, wrote a lovely poem about this incident, a poem which captures its full pathos:

Two lil' guys

On a bright sunny day,

Out in a world

They discover by play.

One bumped the other

The other fell down

And the world turned about

And bumped the bumper down.

"World," cried the bumper,

"I don't understand.

We're both lil' guys

And both need a hand."

The world looked at each

Through enlightened eyes,

Inhaled the wisdom

And hugged both lil' guys.

Children break down the inhibiting walls and uncover hidden wells of gentleness. Danny was distinctive looking, dwarfed and gradually hobbled by Hunter's Syndrome. Once I made the mistake of actually driving in New York City. (I was not a recidivist: I never tried it again.) I was in a parking garage putting Danny back into his car seat. A gruff looking attendant, with a face battered by weather and maybe reddened by too much brew, was watching intently as I put Danny into his seat. The attendant's face emitted no auguries of tenderness. Danny was smiling non-stop as he always did when you were face to face with him. He was hardly aware of what it was you were doing for him, but he delighted in the encounter anyhow. When I finished I approached the attendant who had been watching so I could pay the exorbitant parking fee. With no change of expression the man said: "There'll be no charge sir. Have a good day." I'm sure no one else in New York city parked free that day. Behind that gruff face was a sensitivity that could respond to sorrow with the only gift he had at hand.

Sex Education 101

Kids love surprise: adults don't. Hard charging adults relish predictability. Children dash that and keep us supple. With their surprises, they can turn tedium into delight.

What is duller than driving your car to a gas station to fill up? I taught for a year as the John A. O'Brien chair-holder at the University of Notre Dame. Six-year-old Tommy often came for a few days with me to South Bend. He would sit in the back of the classroom as I lectured, coloring. After one class, I took him with me as I headed into South Bend to gas up.

From his car seat Tommy opened the conversation in a very winsome way, indeed in an entrapping way. "Daddy," said the little boy who had just heard me lecturing, "you know lots of things." I had no problem with that encomium. Having set me up, he continued: "Daddy, I bet you even know what fuck means!"

This was it, the moment I knew was coming. I first warned him that this was a word he should not use with his teachers. He was offended: "I know that!!" "Where did you hear it?" "On the school bus," that major center of American education.

Now I, a sophisticated daddy, knew it was important to answer questions on sex but not to tell too much. It was not the time to go into a description of cunnilingus. So, with perfect paternal grace, I said: "That word refers to the sexual things that people who love one another do together." "Sexual things?" he said, with the excitement that comes with a breakthrough. There was another pause, and I wondered how things were going. "Daddy, do you mean stuff like hugging and kissing and stuff like that?" "Yes," I said, full of both relief and self-congratulation on how deftly I had handled this. I gave him just so much, not too much, textbook perfect.

With that I pulled into the gas station and started filling up the tank. A couple of people pulled up and were standing behind waiting their turn at the pump. Suddenly, the back window of the car started winding down, and Tommy's head appeared. He had a follow-up question and he shouted it with full voice. "Daddy, do some people fuck every day?" What those bystanders thought of this University of Notre Dame daddy professor I will never know. What I could not figure out was why Tom's mind had moved from essence to frequency. I should have answered with Father Merkelbach's frequency limit of three or four times a night but the situation was funny enough already.

When I got back in the car Tom asked: "What are you laughing at, Daddy?" The mature Tommy has since then often joined me in the laugh that he provided with his first steps into sexology.

Chapter Eight
HUMOR HAS THE RIGHT OF WAY

mperors without clothes are commonplace in life, and humor is the *Wunderkind* who calls them on it, pointing out their nakedness. Katzuko and Mizuko came from Japan to Catholic University in Washington. They had sort of converted to Catholicism though they never jettisoned their Buddhist practices or outlooks. They came to theology full of questions with the freshness of the newly arrived and with a whole different backdrop of reference points. In one class the learned professor was explaining the rationale for enforced celibacy for nuns and priests. He was at pains to show that this in no way was meant as a disparagement of married life or sexuality. He insisted: "We consider marriage to be a good, in fact so great a good, that the sacrifice of it is noble." Katzuko's hand went up. Her question: "Do you consider celibacy to be good, Father?" "Yes," he replied, "of course." Then Katzuko's *coup de grace*: "Then why not sacrifice celibacy, Father?"

The professor tut-tutted, unaware that his argument had just been stripped naked, its ridiculosity bared—and all that done, not with the hammer of argument but with a gentle flip of wit.

95

Humor is the only cure for pomposity. That's why the jester is and always was a universal phenomenon. There were jesters "in every court worth its salt, in medieval and Renaissance Europe, in China India, Japan, Russia, America, and Africa. A cavalcade of jesters tumble across centuries and continents, and one could circle the globe tracing their footsteps," as Beatrice Otto puts it. Humor saves people from choking on their own importance and from those stupid ideas that get a lock on the brain. Even the Bible says it's so. Ecclesiastes gives a jolt to pompous intellectuals and economists saying: "They are all emptiness and chasing the wind." How impolite! And how accurate!

Every power center needs a jester. Wall Street needs multiple full-time jesters. Imagine what jesters could do with "sub-prime mortgages" and "derivatives." Oh and what work awaits the jester on our Supreme Court. What fun a jester could have had with *Citizens United*, the decision that declared corporations to be person…you know, persons, like you and me and Harry next door…that kind of person. Would you want your daughter to marry one? The best refutation of that judicial clowning was a cartoon in the *New Yorker* that had a lawyer pleading to the nine great jurists: "When the corporation is tickled, does it not laugh, when it is pricked, does it not bleed?" Summary judgment in a single cartoon! Nothing more left to be said. Five Supreme Court justices symbolically stripped naked, pot bellies and all, and looking so, so silly.

Jesters and comedians are civil servants. I learned this at my mother's knee. My mother, Cassie, believed that where there is no fun, human life decays. From doctor's offices to classrooms, from board rooms to Vatican, White House or Kremlin chambers, there will be fun or failure. That's the Gospel according to Cassie. When she was in her early nineties I went back to relieve my bother Joe, her principal caretaker, to free him for vacation. I was fresh from a conference and I was rhapsodic about it, as was Joe when I reported on it to him. Cassie sat listening as I spoke of the great people and great thoughts of that great conference. After fifteen minutes of listening, Cassie from the couch interjected this indicting question: "Was there *fun* at that conference?" She wouldn't phrase it this way but we knew what the question meant: "if there was no fun there, it was bullshit!"

Thirty years later I don't even remember what conference it was, but I am still quoting Cassie. How lucky I was to be born into a house where humor always had the right of way. Cassie lived her gospel and it saved her a lot of pain. Pain she had when I began being quoted in the press as fighting the pope on issues like birth control. She grew up in an Ireland where many folks knelt around the radio when a speech of the pope, in Italian, was broadcast. To raise a son who would fight the pope was heart-breaking. It hurt me greatly when I was told that someone had met Cassie on the avenue coming from church in tears, tears that my public dissent had caused.

The papers had many stories about "the dissenting priest professors" at Catholic University and elsewhere. Cassie called them "dissenters" with about five *s*'s scorned into the word. That her son was among these "disssssenters" was a blow to her faith and hopes, and it was a sorrow for me to know it.

Fun To The Rescue!

On my father's 83rd birthday, I had my parents down to the Catholic University in Washington for a party. Both parents loved parties and so would attend one even at Catholic University, that den of iniquity from whence dissent was flowing. At the party were all the priest faculty, some dissenters, some not. There were nuns there too, most no longer wearing the long robes. My father, the 83-year-old birthday boy, commented: "First time I ever saw a nun's legs. Nice!"

It was a great party and Cassie was queen of the night. Afterwards in her room, she sat me down to go over with me all the party-goers. Her mission: to identify who were "dissenters" and who were standing with the pope. Her questions ran like this: "The wee man with the pipe, is he a dissenter?" "And the redheaded professor, is he one?" After this process of identification, Cassie leaned back in her chair, took a deep breath and said: "Damned but the dissenters are fun!" She was not about to identify with those taut defenders of papal rectitude. Her summation: "Youse are young," she said, "you'll figure it all out." And so it came to pass that the tears ended and laughter resumed. Thereafter she would at times jocosely refer to me as "Martin," with reference, of course, to that rebellious sixteenth-century German monk. She would ask: "Is Martin coming home tonight?" Our home from then on was often filled with jolly "dissenters."

Surprise

Humor jolts us out of ruts, and surprise is its electrical charge. This is true from Peek-a-boo to Mark Russell, Jon Stewart, and Stephen Colbert. Take the "Abstinence Only" campaign, the latest effort to keep the young folks moral after school. It's the "Just say no to sex" thing that makes no more sense than "Just say no to dandruff." Learned tomes have assaulted it; statistics have embarrassed it. Humor, with its eye-popping surprise, is quicker.

A cartoon in the New Yorker had two college girls sitting in their dorm room looking at an ABSTINENCE ONLY poster. Said one to the other: "The way I see it, there'll be plenty of time for abstinence when I'm married."

The great Mohandas Gandhi, not known as a humorist could be both funny and brilliant at once. *He was asked: "What do you think of Western civilization?" He replied: "That would be a wonderful idea!"* More powerful than a lecture.

The retold joke is not as funny, because the surprise is gone. Another example.

If you have a serious, potentially violent disagreement with someone, walk a mile in his shoes. Then, he is a mile away, and you have his shoes.

Humor, when not debased into ridicule, does not offend. Sacred images can be laughed at with no offense given. The cartoon showed Mary and Joseph at the original Christmas creche scene. The shepherds arrive and see both of them with long faces, looking sad and distraught. A shepherd asked "What's wrong?" Mary replied: "We were hoping for a girl." No harm done.

A Great Notre Dame Football Player

I don't know how good he was on the field or how his athletic career unfolded, but this football player was a great success as a person. One of the times when I was at Notre Dame, Tommy came with me for a few days. He was into arm wrestling then and he would occasionally challenge me. Out of human decency, I would sometimes let him win. It seems that this unduly inflated his self-confidence.

One day we were in the Notre Dame cafeteria having lunch when he spotted a huge young man at a nearby table wearing a tee shirt that said: NOTRE DAME FOOTBALL. He looked the part of a formidable lineman with muscles bulging. Tommy said: "I bet I could arm wrestle him." Without saying a word I went over to the football player and, with a straight face said: "My son wants to challenge you in arm wrestling." With a suppressed smile, he said: "I'd be willing to give it a try." Over he came to our table and the contest commenced. Students at nearby tables saw it and congregated around the table, cheering Tommy, very much in the spirit of the event. At first, the football player started slowly to press Tom's arm down. Then suddenly he weakened and Tom triumphantly slapped his arm down on the table to the loud applause of the students.

The football player said: "I've just got to do more training," and he congratulated the beaming victor.

Tom was gracious in victory. When everything quieted down, Tom leaned over and whispered in my ear—so as not to give offense: "I think that guy is mostly fat." Whatever that guy was, he was mostly great. He was into fun.

Fun with Chinese Condoms

Professor Geling Shang teaches at a university in the bustling city of Shanghai. We worked together when I was president of The Religious Consultation on Population, Reproductive Health and Ethics (www.religiousconsultation.org), a group of progressive, international, scholars of world religions. At one session he mentioned that in the People's Republic of China they were now putting free condoms in motel and hotel drawers alongside the hand cream and shampoo. We were having a very serious conversation that needed a little lightening, so I replied with faux seriousness: "Condoms in motel drawers? We don't do that. We put Bibles there instead. We are convinced that if a couple come to the motel to have sex and find the Bible, they will read that instead."

Keeping a strained straight face professor Shang asked: "Have you any data?"

"Oh, yes, I replied. We have loads and loads of data including the highest unplanned pregnancy rate in the Western World."

It was a funny exchange but what is really funny is the dominant American culture that would go berserk at the very thought of the Chinese policy, a Puritan culture that is more upset by sex than military slaughter. A witty bishop during the Second Vatican Council in the 1960s quipped: "If America had dropped condoms instead of atom bombs on Hiroshima and Nagasaki, the Catholic world would have roared in protest!" Wit as rapier.

Statutory Rape

My son, Danny, even though retarded ,was full of energy in his early years. On Wisconsin wintry days we would often take him to a shopping center where, with man-to-man supervision, he could run a bit. One hazard of this was the water fountain, called in local dialect "a bubbler." Danny loved to turn the water on and watch it splashing quite unaware that other people might be in line behind him. One day I saw him heading for a "bubbler." Just before he or I got there, a young teenage girl in tight-fitting jeans, just coming into her blooming young body, arrived. She bent to drink. At that instant Danny arrived too late to assume control of the bubbler. So, making the best of the situation, Danny reached up and grabbed both of this young lady's buttocks. She bolted up, wheeled around—and saw only me! I had arrived a second too late to prevent Danny's sexual harassment. Before she could call the police, I explained and she saw Danny and understood the sequence of events and Danny's condition. Nervously we both laughed as Danny assumed control of the bubbler. Tragedy and comedy met.

Comedian/Tragedian

It is the oddest of couplings but the tragic and the comic actually do connect. Both tragedy and comedy open minds, one painfully, the other pleasantly. In some strange ways, the two are linked. The tearless will also be the laughless, and vice versa. James Lynwood Walker suggests that Jews and African Americans who have encountered an undue share of the tragic, have both produced "cogent thinkers and sensitive comics." With admitted bias I would add the Irish to this listing.

Dick Gregory in his heyday showed all this. In a way that teeters between comedy and tragedy he used to tell audiences why, as the title of his first book, he used that dreaded name *Nigger*. I watched him tell an audience of whites how black parents fear the first time their children will hear that mordant word and discover the venom it contains and the wounding things it is saying about them and their moms and dads. If a pin dropped at that moment, everyone would have heard it. Said Gregory: "So I called my book *Nigger* so that when my kids first heard that terrible word they'd say delightedly: 'Isn't that cool! Somebody's talking about daddy's book!'" The audience laughed but could as easily have cried, as this comedian-trage-dian also played the exorcist, driving out the demons that possessed that word now belatedly, slowly en route to burial.

Gregory, who had that white audience rolling with laughter could sud-denly bring us to tears. Like other black comedians in the sixties, he often used the N word as part of their effort to defang it. We in his Catholic Uni-versity audience didn't know what was coming when he said: "The prob-lem with us Niggers is memory. We remember too much." He then told of his grandmother who knew a woman who had been a slave. Her master used to sell off the healthy babies of his slaves. They brought a good price since they could be reared and trained to slavery more easily. The only child they could keep was a "deformed" baby. Gregory's grandmother said the slave woman had lost four children that way. Sold off for a life of slavery somewhere else. During her next pregnancy, she prayed: "Oh Lord, make my baby deformed."

Gregory paused when he said that and then, said softly, "Think of that prayer, White Folks."

Then, he said, the baby was born with only part of one arm, and the woman said: "Thank you, Lord Jesus, I can keep my baby, I can keep my baby!" After a moment, Gregory broke the absolute silence of his audience saying, "now think of that prayer, and remember it."

The Fiddler of Dooney

Where humor is revered, poetry prospers. Not surprising since their mission is the same, to peek beyond the obvious. William Butler Yeats talks of humor and its primacy and does it in his poem The Fiddler of Dooney where merriment outranks piety.

When I play on my fiddle in Dooney,

Folk dance like a wave of the sea;

My cousin is priest in Kivbarnet,

My brother in Moharabuiee.

I passed my brother and cousin:

They read in their book of prayer;

I read in my book of songs

I bought at the Sligo fair.

When we come to the end of time,

To Peter sitting in state,

He will smile on the three old spirits,

But [he'll] call me first through the gate;

For the good are always the merry,

Save by an evil chance,

And the merry love the fiddle

And the merry love to dance:

And when the folk there spy me,

They will all come up to me,

With 'Here is the fiddler of Dooney!'

And they'll dance like a wave of the sea.

CHAPTER NINE
ON ROILING BISHOPS AND
GETTING GERALDINE FERRARO IN TROUBLE

Now I know "getting a girl in trouble" used to refer to pregnancy and let me make this perfectly clear. I did not get Geraldine Ferraro pregnant. We did not have that kind of a relationship. We did have breakfast together, but even that was not a *tete a tete*. There were about 30 members of Congress there and some other professors and activists from Catholics For Choice. It was all very above board but it still got Representative Ferraro into a peck of trouble. She was trying to help out members of Congress who were getting badgered on the abortion issue. She knew the issue was not as simple as the hierarchy made it out to be and she asked me to address that.

I told her in advance that I would explain that the Catholic view on abortion "was not monolithic." There was a pro-choice view alongside the no-choice view and that many distinguished theologians throughout history, including one saint, St. Antoninus, held a pro-choice view. In her invitation to the members of Congress she wrote using my words "that the

Catholic position on abortion is not monolithic and that there can be a range of personal and political responses to the issue."

Later Ms. Ferraro was the vice-presidential candidate running with Walter Mondale. One day she was campaigning out in Iowa and the press came to her saying that Cardinal John O'Connor of New York appeared on the steps of St. Patrick's Cathedral and denounced her for saying that the Catholic view on abortion "was not monolithic." (O'Connor's view was paleolithic.) Ms. Ferrraro was befuddled. When had she made such a statement!

Well it seems some Republican rascal gave the cardinal a copy of the invitation she had sent to the members saying that the breakfast briefing would show Catholics as not "monolithic" on abortion. The press researched it and found that she was quoting me. When I arrived at Marquette that morning (I'll explain in a moment how I got to Marquette) there were a dozen phone messages in my mail box asking me to call The New York Times, the Washington Post, and the major television networks. In a letter to the New York Times on September 16, I said that the Archbishop's wrath should have been directed to me since it was my view that "the Catholic position on abortion is not monolithic." I added: "Even if the bishops are monolithic on some issues, it does not mean that the church is." That did not go over well with those fellows who dress up in red robes and wear miters.

Banned in Boston, etc.

So Geraldine Ferraro was now not the only one in trouble. My pro-choice views were now public, very, very public. The immediate fallout was a remarkable anomaly: within days, I found myself in this anomalous situation: while employed at one Catholic university (Marquette) I was fired by four other Catholic universities.

At first blush, my relationship to five universities all at once might seem a tad complicated but it's not. During that summer four Catholic institutions of higher learning had invited me to give workshops: Boston College, Villanova University, The College of St. Scholastica in Duluth and St. Martin's College in Lacey, Washington. All four of the institutions had contracted with me; they really wanted me. Suddenly, when the Geraldine Ferraro story hit the presses, they really did not want me. In fact, they unwanted me so much they were willing to pay me not to come. I was making more money for not speaking that summer than my colleagues were making for speaking. At that moment I could identify with those farmers who were paid to plow their crops under.

The American Association of University Professors (AAUP) appointed a special committee to study this deluge of dis-invitations. Their report said: "With a reputation as an outspoken and challenging authority on moral and social issues, Professor Maguire was frequently in demand as a speaker, particularly on Catholic college and university campuses." That popularity screeched to a halt in the summer of 1985. The AAUP report criticized all four institutions for their lack of academic freedom but the institutions stayed firm. A group of spirited "pro-life" people picketed Marquette University calling for my head. (A local TV station called telling me the picketers were carrying a well made sign saying: "FIRE MAGUIRE PRIEST OF DEATH." The station asked for my reaction and I commented that I would like that sign for my den after they finished with it. I never got it but I understand they made further use of it so there was no waste.

An Ouster and Then a Happy Landing

Now let me get back to how in my odyssey I went from Catholic University in Washington to Marquette University in Milwaukee. The Catholic University you recall, was able to keep the professors who defended condoms, but they choked on "the sanctity of marriage." Cheers for the AAUP that defended the professors and more cheers for Cravath, Swaine and Moore, the prestigious New York law firm that defended us without charging us a penny.

107

But insult was added to injury when I announced that I was going to leave the priesthood to marry. Oh no, they said, that was seen as an unspeakable crime and Catholic University would have none of it.

Showing how complicated it was to wage theology in those days, it took another law firm to get this settled. The story hit the press that I, although tenured, would be fired for getting married. The Washington Post carried the story. It also got an interesting headline from a left wing paper called *The Quicksilver Times*. "PIGS SACK PRIEST." The publicity got the attention of a first rate law firm in Washington called Dickstein, Shapiro and Gallligan. (With two Jews and an Irishman, how could I lose.) They offered to represent me on a *pro bono* basis simply because they found my ouster unconscionable.

With that kind of legal muscle behind me, Catholic University got the shivers and decided to settle. I required two things to settle: enough money to make a down-payment on my Milwaukee home, and a formal "laicization" from the Vatican. This would end my priestly status and give me respectable standing as a layman. Marquette was interested in me but they wanted that "laicization" to make me kosher.

Wonder of wonders, I got it all. With the litigating power of Dickstein, Shapiro and Galligan in the background, they prevailed on the Vatican to grant my formal laicization. In a revealing irony, I got the writ of laicization handed to me not by the local church official, but by the lawyers of Dickstein, Shapiro and Galligan. The lawyers knew I needed it to get my position at Marquette and they would not settle until they had it in hand. You couldn't call it a religious moment. You could call it a piece of hard-nosed bargaining from a noble firm that knew how to do it.

Lunch With Clarence Thomas

Breakfast with Geraldine Ferraro was fine; lunch with Clarence Thomas

108

was something else. So how did it come to be? When in the course of human events it came to pass that a second-rate movie actor named Ronald Reagan had become president of the United States of America, I was asked to speak at the Drake University Law School. It was a well organized conference with spokespersons from the Right and from the Left, including some people from the administration of said Reagan. My talk was on affirmative action, but in my talk I lambasted the Reagan administration for, among other things, taking a vegetable out of school lunches on the grounds that the kids already had ketchup and ketchup was veggie enough for them. I was not gentle for no gentleness was due.

Afterwards I was taken to lunch only to discover that someone with a wry sense of humor had decided I would dine with Clarence Thomas, then head of the Equal Employment Opportunity Commission, an agency he was slowly putting to sleep. With him were two of his assistants. Clarence and his associates had been present for my speech and I could see from the chilly faces that this was not going to be a "hail fellows well met" moment. Clarence opened by saying he hated "all this Republican bashing." With a straight face he proclaimed that you have to make it in life on your own and not expect government to take you there! Talk about *cojones!* He, the beneficiary of affirmative action, was sitting there claiming Horatio Alger virtue.

He had other complaints. Obviously my talk had not sweetened his mood. He was resentful about how he and the other African American Clarence in the Reagan administration, Clarence Pendleton, were treated. Pendleton, like Thomas, hated affirmative action and things like that so Reagan made Pendleton chair of the U.S. Commission on Civil Rights. Thomas indignantly remarked that "the two Clarences" were referred to as the "HN's," (House plus the N word) of the Reagan administration. I thought the criticism was well taken but I did not further foul the mood by saying so.

My comments were taking the veggies out of kids' lunches was definitely sticking in the craw of these not so gentle gentlemen. One of Clarence's assistants took me on about the kids' lunches. He told me that it was a very complicated decision. "So complicated," I countered, "that it could not be corrected by a simple phone call saying: 'Give the kids back their veggie!'" I then got a lecture on how liberals don't understand the challenges of governing. "Maybe not," I said, "but we're not bad at spotting meanness."

Clarence Thomas and his men made an impression on me at this jousting lunch. I remember it was St. Patrick's Day and I was going home to go to a party at Mary Kelly's. I was thinking as I burped my way onto the plane (Republicans affect my digestion), it will take a lot of Irish whiskey to wash out the taste of this experience. On the plane I wondered what plans the Republicans had for this Clarence Thomas fellow. Big plans it seems. Clarence is a Catholic of the right wing variety (there is such a thing as left wing Catholicism). He is now part of a Catholic *coup d'etat* on the Supreme Court, six Catholics including the Chief Justice. How far we have come from "Catholics Need Not Apply." Catholics now can have the last word on the law of the land. And five of those Catholics are of the right wing variety, Thomas, Scalia, and Alito of the rabidly so. Only one represents the Catholic social justice tradition. Justice Sonia Sotomayor.

It makes you wonder. Could you imagine having five conservative Muslims or Orthodox Jews on the Supreme Court, including one of them as Chief Justice. It would not be viewed with similar complacency. Talk about having arrived!

An All-Too-Close Encounter of a Third Kind

When I met Cardinal Joseph Ratzinger in the piazza of St. Peter's, he did not invite me for breakfast, lunch, or dinner. But he did make clear that he disliked me even more than Clarence Thomas did. Meeting Pope Benedict XVI when he was still just a lowly cardinal was a nice occasion. At least I enjoyed it. It seemed less fun to him. It was certainly fun for my nine-year-old son who was with me.

110

It was a beautiful day in early September. Rome's terrible summer hear, *la caldura*, had abated. Pope John Paul II was flying in by helicopter from his summer hideaway in Castel Gandolfo. The airborne pope first circled over the square, landed in the Vatican gardens, and then emerged into St. Peter's piazza in the open pope-mobile he used at that time. The Pope John Paul II who was at heart a real ham, was beaming and waving and flashing blessings. We managed to get Tom a spot at the fence where the pope would pass by. When the pope saw Tom, the only kid in that part of the crowd, he ordered the pope-mobile to stop and he reached down and shook hands with Tom. That was not bad, but there was more to come.

After the audience, when the pope left, we were leaving the piazza when I spotted Cardinal Ratzinger walking to his office, smiling benignly at the crowd of the faithful. His office was right next to St. Peter's. It used to be called Office of the Inquisition. Ratzinger's job there was as the enforcer of orthodoxy; he was to ride herd on adventuresome theologians, and he took to his work with zest. As soon as I spotted him, I told my son to get his camera and follow me. We caught up to the cardinal and I asked him in Italian if I could take a picture of him with my son. He replied in perfect English: "But of course." He posed amiably and I got some fine pictures of Cardinal Ratzinger and Tom in his Milwaukee Brewers T shirt.

I saw the three faces of Ratzinger that day. This first face was smiling, beaming really. He was among the faithful from whom he could expect only homage and here was me, obviously a pious father with his son. He asked me if I was enjoying my "pilgrimage" to Rome. With the pictures successfully lodged in my camera, I confess to feeling a sense of what the Irish call "divilment" rising in me, and I replied: "Yes, especially since I am a Catholic theologian." The mood changed and the second face of Ratzinger replaced the first! A theologian? This put me squarely on his turf. I was now not just a pious parent, I was one of those his job was to police. Out of pure egotism, I decided to play one more card. I said: "My name is Daniel Maguire." He lost it. Face # 3: *furious*. "What?" he shouted loudly and angrily. "You are Daniel Maguire!"

My son, misinterpreting his outburst asked me: "Why is he so surprised?" The cardinal stood glaring at me. I broke the grim silence saying "My son's name is Thomas. I named him for Thomas Aquinas." Ratzinger had a good recovery: "Perhaps someday he will be as great a theologian as Thomas Aquinas." I replied: "He is already beginning to ask some good questions." (I should have said: if he's that good, you fellows will condemn him—as they did condemn Thomas Aquinas.)

Over lunch my son asked: "Why didn't he say I might be as great a theologian as my Daddy?" Tom had a point.

The picture came out beautifully and as I sit at my desk today, Cardinal Ratzinger, now Pope Benedict XVI, smiles down on me approvingly, seeming to encourage me in my work. Pope Benedict is a man who didn't age well. At the time of Vatican Council II he was a liberal and a bit of a worry to the inquisitors of that day. He would not give the last word to the pope, saying conscience had priority, in line with Cardinal John Henry Newman who famously said that he would toast the pope but would toast his conscience first. In Ratzinger's own youthful words: "Over the pope as the expression of the binding claim of ecclesiastical authority there still stands one's own conscience, which must be obeyed before all else, if necessary even against the requirement of ecclesiastical authority. This emphasis on the individual, whose conscience confronts him with a supreme and ultimate tribunal, and one which in the last resort is beyond the claim of external social groups, even of the official Church, also establishes a principle in opposition to increasing totalitarianism." "One's own conscience" standing "over the pope." Nice! But, oh my, how he changed.

Anyhow, it was flattering to know that the Cardinal knew my work even if he didn't like it. It's a shame he doesn't like my writing, but I just have to live with it. In fact, if he approved of me, I'd have to worry. So we have a truce. He doesn't bother me and I only occasionally bother him.

The Weight of 270 Bishops

Bishops live in a bubble, and that really is not healthy. They associate with one another and with right wing theologians who are equally conservative and boxed in. It's like breathing recycled air. Once again, unhealthy. Living that way would do no harm socially if they would just shut up. After all, they are not theologians; most could not pass a graduate exam in theology...undergraduate? maybe. They are administrators, lobbyists, pastors, but not professional theologians. And yet they do play that role on TV and in the press.

There was a time back during the Second Vatican Council in the 1960s when bishops and theologians were together a lot. In Rome they would go to dinner or chat over coffee during the Council and it was nice. Bishops starting making more sense. But then they retreated back into their bubble. Now they are embarrassing themselves, most recently arguing loudly that their "religious freedom" gives them the right to violate the religious freedom of other people Working from their tax-exempt properties they try to change the nation's policies and laws to curtail the reproductive rights of all citizens and to further stigmatize same-sex couples. They can't control their priests' sexual behavior but they would like to get the whole country by the short hairs.

Put Up or Shut Up

The year was 2006 and it was the merry month of June. After years of complaining about bishops behaving badly, I decided to go right into their bubble and talk to them. I wrote a letter to each and every one of them. I was polite. I began saying "given the great divide that exists in the contemporary Church between bishops and theologians, I think that communication, even if it leads to little agreement, is a human good." Quite diplomatic.

I then said that they overemphasize issues like abortion and same-sex marriage where there are good religious authorities on both sides of those questions. I said that their voices were needed and could be very helpful on issues like "our nation's militarism, neglect of the world's poor, racism, sexism and the wrecking of the earth's ecology through greed."

So how many bishops replied to me? Three. Two were polite. Bishop Thomas Doran of Rockford, Illinois and Bishop Jerome Listecki of La Crosse Wisconsin. They expressed disagreement but they were nice about it. The third response came from the Milwaukee archbishop, Timothy Dolan, now cardinal Dolan in New York. Dolan was not nice. He was rabid. He said everything I said was "totally at odds with clear Church teaching. Then he got into name-calling; my teaching was "preposterous and disingenuous." ("Disingenuous" is the euphemism for "liar, liar pants on fire.") Dolan had already told his priests that I was not to be allowed to speak on any topic in any parish in Milwaukee ever, so I sensed he was not keen on my work. Fine. I wasn't keen on his either.

From the other 267 bishops, nothing. But they were thinking about it. They thought for nine months, the length of a pregnancy. Then the other shoe—in fact 267 other shoes—dropped in March 2007. That was a nice surprise. Five pages, single space, with 24 footnotes arrived from the "Committee on Doctrine of the United States Conference of Catholic Bishops." I no longer felt neglected or ignored. It was signed by eight bishops and one cardinal, Cardinal Avery Dulles. I could not file it as "fan mail." They weren't enthused about my message. The *New York Times* headline read "Bishops Denounce Writings of a Catholic Theologian." A spokesperson for the U.S. Conference of Catholic bishops said that the response to me "carried the weight of all 270 U.S. bishops, not just the nine signatories." (When an Irish priest friend heard this he wrote me a sympathy note saying: "Given the girth of most of those men, Dan, that is a terrible burden for you to bear.)

Of all the bishops it was Cardinal Dulles who was most offended by what I wrote. In my letter I had quoted some of the liberal things he said when he was a younger scholar. Like Ratzinger, Dulles later in life took a hard turn to the right, and like Ratzinger he too was then made a cardinal. Dulles told the press that the most galling thing I wrote to the bishops was that they were just one voice among many in the church, not the guys with the last word on everything. Good, I thought, at least they understood me.

I didn't write to the bishops again. I decided this crowd was not ripe for dialogue since they are still inpenetrable and getting worse.

Now how did Marquette University react to all this hullabaloo? Not badly. They defended my academic freedom, and that is all one can ask. Marquette has heard a lot from my right wing booing section over the years. An assistant to the president told me that when he got this job he received a two-page list of his duties. One of his duties was "to answer complaints about Professor Maguire." They even developed a form letter saying I was the price you have to pay to be a real university. At a cocktail party one time one of the vice presidents told me that they get a lot of letters saying they will not give another dime to the university until I am removed. He said they did a check and found that most of them had never given a dime anyhow. It was friendly of him to tell me that.

My wife got a whiff of how common this complaint was. She is a doctor. One day in the doctors' lounge she was sitting near two older doctors who had come in for a lecture. They didn't know her and she didn't know them. It turns out they were Marquette alums. One asked the other if he had gotten the recent appeal for funds from Marquette. The other replied that he had. He then said he responded to the letter by writing back that

115

he would never contribute to Marquette again until they got rid of that professor. He could not remember the name of the professor. My wife, sitting at a nearby table, shouted over, "Maguire.

"Yes, the doctor said, that's it and he thanked her and they continued grousing about me.

Edie finished her coffee and as she left she said: "Professor Maguire is my husband and he teaches more Christian values than all those right-wingers you support." To use one of my mother's phrases, the two doctors, quite taken aback, sat there "like ducks looking at thunder."

Weep Not For Me

No one survives as a social critic without good luck and happy surprises. I tell my students that if they see me bow a bit when I pass the Raynor Memorial Library on Marquette's campus there is a reason for that. After I was very publicly ejected from The Catholic University of America for perpetrating matrimony, Marquette hired me. Shortly after I began teaching there, the president of the university, John Raynor, S.J., was seeking funds from a local philanthropist, a man who could be fairly described as an idiosyncratic conservative Catholic fanatic. Fr. Raynor was rebuffed at the very start of his pitch by the question: "Why should I give you anything when you just hired this liberal ex-priest?" Raynor's reply, related to me by Quentin Quade. the executive vice president of Marquette was: "Maguire's head is not for sale. He has the credentials we were looking for." I'm happy to report that he got the money he was asking for.

And here is the lovely part of this story: both Raynor and Quade were conservative and would disagree with me on most things, but both held to the university ideal of "many minds competing freely together." They may have swallowed very hard but they always defended me. (There had to be a wave of winces at my university when Pope John Paul II first visited the United States. *People Magazine* did an article on " nine people the pope does not want to meet," and I was one of them.) Vice President Quade, in one of his public statements defending academic freedom, referred to me as "the occasional anomaly" that must be defended if a university is to be true to its mission. I've been called worse. Father Raynor, who was a genuinely pious man, may well have often prayed that I would shut up on certain issues that roiled his generous conservative constituencies, but he proved himself a leader with true academic grit. When he retired, *The Milwaukee Journal* editorialized on his many achievements including his defense of "maverick theologian Daniel C. Maguire." They later did an editorial headed "Why Marquette Doesn't Muzzle Maguire," in which they praised Marquette's record on academic freedom.

CHAPTER TEN
A BETTER WAY TO DIE

Woody Allen said he is not afraid of dying; he just doesn't want to be there when it happens. He also turned his attention to the "eternity" some think awaits us after we get the dying done. He warned: "Eternity is a really, really long time, especially toward the end."

OK, death is serious but we might as well laugh at it. There are a lot of afterlife hopes out there, but death remains the impenetrable mystery. The afterlifers think death does not happen. It just looks like it happens. You look dead and after a few days—unless somebody does something fast—you will smell dead but, it is the instinctive hope of many—maybe most—that you're not really dead. You just went bye-byes and left your body behind.

There are no witnesses to an afterlife in spite of all the ghost stories and myths of resurrections. There are also stories of everyone from the Caesars to Jesus who, after they died, ascended into heaven without ever going into orbit. My uncle Dan departed from Christian orthodoxy and didn't buy any of this: "no one ever came back," he said dismissively...shocking every one of his Irish Catholic family and friends.

So here we are, the only animal that knows it is going to die and we have borne that privileged information with uneven grace. But cope with mortality we all must. I had a series of mentors to instruct me on dying. In fact, I was involved in my uncle Dan's death, in a big way; I actually helped accelerate it. This is the same Uncle Dan I was named for, the one who didn't believe in an afterlife.

Here's the story.

Uncle Dan had come to spend his final days at our house. His heart was failing and he was in frequent pain. When the pain hit, he cried out with the strength of a young man. The doctor opined that his pressure was so low that organs would start collapsing and this triggered sharp shocks of pain in various parts of his body. One night I helped him to bed and gave him the two green capsules prescribed for sleep. He slept for 45 minutes and then the terrible pains struck and he screamed. I called the doctor from the phone in his room. He could hear the cries of pain. He asked if I had given the two pills and I said I had, just 45 minutes ago. More cries of pain. Then a slow deliberate directive from the doctor on the phone. "Give him two more." "Could he tolerate two more?" I asked. The doctor did not answer my question. Instead he repeated firmly: "Give him two more." I did. The pain subsided, he slept, and he never woke again.

When I found him dead in the morning, the doctor came to pronounce death, and there was a wordless conversation between the doctor who made a moral decision the night before and the moralist who had never before seen up close the wisdom of the Irish saying: "there are worse things than dying." More of that terrible, painful, hopeless living would have been worse than dying for Uncle Dan.

Doubleday published my first book; it was called *Death by Choice*, defending deliberate actions to accelerate the dying process, mercy death.

Should uncle Dan and his doctor have been listed as co-authors? Once again, theory is, to a significant degree, autobiography.

Mrs. Sweeney: Choreographing Death

Not all cultures are as stupid about dying as the dominant American culture. We still pay undertakers to paint bodies to make them look alive when they are obviously, awesomely dead. And in what is called cryonics, some wackos try freezing the body in hopes of a medical resurrection someday. Happily, cremation is now more accepted as a way of facing facts.

I am happy that in my travels I got to experience other healthier ways of dying. Mrs. Sweeney in Glenties, Co. Donegal was very good at it. I hope I can die her way. It was really, really cool.

My parents and I were in Ireland visiting old friends in Glenties. We came to see Mrs. Sweeney who we had heard was dying. We visited with her briefly in her room. For me, something was jarring about those minutes with this dying woman. Her family were all there, but no one was pretending that Sadie was not dying, which would be the polite American thing to do. No one was saying "don't worry, Mom, you'll be out picking the spuds in the spring." No. There would be no more springs for Mrs. Sweeney and there was not a trace of denial in that room. There was visible grief that she was soon going to be leaving them, but the lack of denial made the event seem an un-American activity. To my young American mind the amenities of denial were being denied her, and surely they were.

We then all went downstairs to do some typically Irish things, talking and drinking. The local doctor was among us and it worried me slightly that he seemed already to have, as the Irish say, "more than a drop taken." After an hour or so of this, a daughter of Mrs. Sweeney rushed into the room and announced: "Mom wants you to come up now and start the

Rosary. She is dying." We went up and in the middle of that ancient Catholic prayer, Mrs. Sweeney did what she was about.

It was baffling. How did Mrs. Sweeney know she was dying? She had never done it before. Only later could I appreciate how she had what the ancients called the *ars moriendi*, the art of dying well. She orchestrated her final moments. First of all, as a decent Irish woman she did not break up the party downstairs too soon. Who would want to die with that on your conscience? But when the time came, she knew it, and she surrounded herself with her family and the symbols of her faith and departed with serenity.

But still the question lingered. How did Mrs. Sweeney know that the moment of death was upon her?

I took my wonderment back to Rome with me and mentioned it to an Irish priest, Patty Wallace. In a very Irish style, he responded to my story with one of his own. (And by the way, let me make one thing perfectly clear: all Irish stories are true. It's just that some of them are a lot truer than others.) It seems there was an old friend of his in Limerick who was dying. Some of his buddies came to say good bye. They didn't come to pretend he wasn't dying. They came to talk of the great times they had together. It was a "do you remember this?" and "do you remember that?" sort of chat. After a little talk, the dying man turned to his son and said, "Jamie, pour the men a wee drink." (It is *de rigeur* to refer to Irish drinks as "wee.") Jamie did as directed and then turned to his Dad and asked: "Will you have a wee one, Dad?" With a disappointed frown the father responded: "Ach, no, Jamie, sure I don't want to be meeting the Lord with the smell of the drink on my breath."

He was dying. Nobody was denying that and when you know you are dying you should observe all the amenities. And he thought it was best to be stone sober.

Now I think his theology was a bit defective there, from a Catholic sort of view. The idea that God would object to someone having a wee drop with friends, dying or not, made no Catholic sense.

He seemed to think that coming face to face with Jesus after death would be like meeting his stern parish priest in the confessional—where you would definitely not want to be blowing alcohol fumes through the wire mesh. Bible scholars could have consoled this dying man with a merrier view of Jesus and the Bible. After all, the psalmist thanks God for "wine to gladden [people's] hearts." (Ps. 104:13-18) Jesus' first reported miracle at Cana was making more wine for people at a wedding party where people had already had "more than a drop taken." Jesus frequented dinner parties as he went about his mission. As Dominican priest and Bible scholar Albert Nolan writes: "These dinner parties were such a common feature of Jesus' life that he could be accused of being a drunkard and a glutton." Catholic scholar Joseph Grassi adds: "Unlike the Baptist, Jesus drank wine and alcohol at the homes and 'taverns' of the day." More remarkable yet, the gospels of Matthew, Mark and Luke all report Jesus right before his death looking forward to having a drink in the kingdom of God. (Matt. 26:29; Mark 14:25; Luke 22:18) "I tell you this: never again shall I drink from the fruit of the vine until that day when I drink it anew with you in the kingdom of my Father." In other words, if there is a heaven, the first thing Jesus would do when he got there is have a drink. That's nice, and it segues beautifully into

JIGGLEDEEGREEN

Just think of all the ink that has been spilled imagining life after death. Catholics could match anyone in conjuring up afterlife scenarios. Generally ancient Jews spoke about the dead going to *Sheol*, but *Sheol*, seems to have been little more than a metaphor for the grave writ large. It was not a jolly prospect and there was certainly nothing heavenly about it. Christians took to afterlife prospects with gusto. Their goriest and least admirable prospect was hell. No wonder that word features so prominently in modern cussing. Hell was presented as unending fiery torture, the last word in cruel and unusual punishment. In the Middle Ages some thought the volcano on Mount Etna was the entrance into hell. Scary! And not only did you scorch, there was no end to the scorching. Life on earth had time limits: life in hell had none. Apparently, infinite combustibility was a capacity you picked up upon dying. Nobody has it pre-mortem. Ask Joan of Arc and Giordano Bruno and any of the poor burnt witches.

But no end to hell's torture? That's mean. Wouldn't you say that a few million years of scorching might be enough even for an Adolph Hitler? You have to ask what kind of a God would ask you to love him "with all your heart and all your soul and all your mind" and then add that if you did not do that, he will fry your ass for all eternity? The hellfire thing was imagination run amok. (A modern cartoonist suggested a worse fate than eternal fire: assignment as a tele-marketer for all eternity. Point well taken.)

In the thirteenth century, Christians softened the hell bit by creating an alternative called Purgatory. Purgatory was a half-way house between life on earth and heaven. It purged you, cleansed you to get you ready for heaven. It was still rough stuff, and some thought Mount Etna might also be the entrance into Purgatory, so it was no cake walk.

Heaven, on the contrary, had no flames. There you would enjoy what was called "the beatific vision." This meant that you would look at God 24/7—no other pastimes permitted—and this would make you supremely happy. Actually, it sounds a little boring.

Unbaptized babies presented a problem for the scholars. They had no personal sins and so were not candidates for hell or purgatory but they lacked baptism, the passport to heaven. They had to be put somewhere, so the theologians created Limbo. Even the conservative Pope Benedict XVI had decided that "limbo" is, after all, only a dance where one tries to bend back under an extended pole and it is not a grim reservation for deceased unbaptized babies.

Help is on the Way

And so it came to pass, again in Glenties, Co. Donegal, Ireland, that a seer arose. She was a woman of marginal intelligence and little schooling who had been taught the post-mortem prospects then envisioned in Catholicism. Somehow, she was unimpressed with this picturing of the afterlife and decided that the listing was incomplete if not downright inaccurate. There was, she told the priests, another place out there—and she was quite sure of this—and its name was Jiggledeegreen.

She had detailed information on life—more properly afterlife—in Jiggledeegreen. Nobody was perfect there. Most had goofed up morally in lots of ways and none dreamed of going to join the choir of the perfect singing God's praises and looking at God non-stop in heaven. Instead in Jiggledeegreen everybody was having a ball. There was lots of dancing—Irish dancing to be sure—and story-telling, and all around good times. Tea was always available and of course you could always have a wee drink. No "beatific vision" but lots of beatific story-telling.

It was this woman's parish priest, Father Arthur McCloone, who told me of this eschatological envisioning, and I am pleased to report that this priest did absolutely nothing to dissuade this woman regarding her take on the afterlife. If this was whimsy, he thought, it is a very consoling whimsy deserving a "do not disturb." And anyhow it sounded pretty much like Jesus' idea of having a post-mortem drink. Of course, Jesus was talking about wine. As a scholar I must note that Jesus in his entire life, never had a drop of Irish whiskey. More's the pity.

What You Can Learn About Living While Dying

Sometimes tragedy is the only teacher who can get through to us. When I wrote my book *Death By Choice* defending mercy death, I was on a television show with another author Orville Kelly who wrote a book called *Make Today Count*. Over lunch he told me his story. He had been an executive in the newspaper business. He described his business self as "aggressive." He said he would stomp his way up the ladder of success. He did however have a serious phobia. He was afraid of death, would go out of his way to avoid wakes and funerals. The dying thing thoroughly spooked him.

He started having pains in his stomach and back and he went to his doctor to get that taken care of. Tests were done and he came back for the results. His doctor was ominously uneasy. The news was obviously bad. Terminal cancer with only a short time of living left. He plunged into depression. Death that he so feared was now inside of him and was his master.

After some weeks in the darkness of despair, he woke one morning feeling good and even hungry. Birds were singing, a bright day was dawning. The thought struck him: "make today count." That was the name of a movement he started, and the name of his book. He found other people under the same medical sentence and discovered that together they could not just comfort one another but could laugh again. When I met him, he was giving dozens of talks a year and was collaborating with Dr. Elizabeth Kubler Ross in her mission to teach a death-shy culture how to die.

At this lunch he made this most memorable comment. He said that since he got cancer, he had become a different kind of person, concerned for others, finding his fulfillment in helping and relating to people. From everything I later learned, I think he was being too hard on himself. But he insisted: "if I had a choice to going back to being the kind of person I was without cancer or having the cancer and being what I have become, I would have to choose the cancer." Happiness is good medicine. I read of his death a couple of years later; he had cheated the doctor's prognosis by at least two years. I had met a great man that day at lunch. His short valedictory to the world he left was "make today count." He inscribed my copy of his book, saying, "Keep up the fight—and don't forget to 'make today count' in your own life."

When my son Danny was diagnosed at twenty-two months with the prediction he would die at around ten, we learned the art of being in his present and making each day count. Danny always tasted the tea of the moment and taught us to do the same as his lovely life began to fade slowly away.

At the time of the diagnosis, Dr. Allen Crocker, an expert in Hunter's syndrome offered us, along with the fearsome prognosis, these gentle words: "Danny will need a lot of love along the way but when it is over, you'll say that you would never have missed having him with you." Our very last words to Danny in his eulogy were these: "We would never have missed out on you, Danny! Not for the whole world!"

Made in the USA
San Bernardino, CA
14 August 2013